5.00

Dad,

I have no idea who Justin is - but I'm sure this book is as good as the rest. Happy Father's Day 2003!

Love,
Laura + Shaun

D0967827

# "And Then the Shark Told Justin..."

# "And Then the Shark Told Justin..."

## A Collection of the Best True Golf Stories Ever Told

DON WADE
Foreword by Nancy Lopez

CB
CONTEMPORARY BOOKS

**Library of Congress Cataloging-in-Publication Data**

Wade, Don.
 "And then the Shark told Justin . . ." : a collection of the best
true golf stories ever told / Don Wade.
  p.   cm.
 Includes index.
 ISBN 0-8092-2505-0
 1. Golf—Anecdotes.  I. Title.
GV967.W265   2001
796.352—dc21                                    00-22960
                                                CIP

Cover design by Todd Petersen
Cover photograph by Steven Szurlej
Illustrations by Paul Szep

Published by Contemporary Books
A division of NTC/Contemporary Publishing Group, Inc.
4255 West Touhy Avenue, Lincolnwood (Chicago), Illinois 60712-1975 U.S.A.
Copyright © 2001 by Don Wade
Printed in the United States of America
International Standard Book Number: 0-8092-2505-0

01 02 03 04 05 06 LB 18 17 16 15 14 13 12 11 10 9 8 7 6 5 4 3 2

For Julia, Ben, Darcy, and Andy

# CONTENTS

# FOREWORD

Fourteen years ago (could it possibly be that long ago!) Don Wade and I collaborated on a book. We had a great time and produced a book that you can still find in the stores. So when Don asked if I'd write the Foreword for this book, I was more than happy to do it.

This book is the eighth in a series that began with *"And Then Jack Said to Arnie . . ."*, and they are great fun to read. Most of the stories are humorous, but, all in all, the books cover every aspect of the game. I don't think there's anything in any of these books that will help you lower your score, but as the late Dave Marr once said, if you have friends or loved ones who don't understand why golf is such a special game, have them read these books—then they'll get it.

Golf is a game that really lends itself to storytelling because you have all that time walking between shots or waiting to tee off—and then, of course, after the round. Plus, interesting things just seem to happen on the golf course.

Having known Don for all these years, I know how much he loves the game and the people who play it. That love is captured in these books. If the game means a lot to you, too, I know you'll enjoy this book and the seven that came before it.

Enjoy.

—Nancy Lopez

# ACKNOWLEDGMENTS

Sometimes in this life, you just get lucky. Certainly, there's an element of luck in the fact that so many people have enjoyed and supported this series of books since the publication of *"And Then Jack Said to Arnie . . . "* in 1991.

But the real luck involves the people who have helped make these books so successful, and I'd like to thank them for their help and their friendship.

Having grown up in Concord, Massachusetts, I've been a fan of Paul Szep's work since the 1960s, when he came south from Canada to inflict misery and pain on the usual suspects, while bringing joy and a measure of revenge to the rest of us. Szeppy's editorial cartoons in the *Boston Globe* have earned him two Pulitzer Prizes and millions of admirers. I'm one of his biggest fans, both for his work and for his great and enduring friendship.

Steve Szurlej and I have been friends for some twenty years, dating back to our early days at *Golf Digest*. He's one of the best photographers in the business, whether he's shooting the action at a tournament, getting just the right shot of a golf course, or making visual sense of yet another arcane instruction story. Steve is responsible for the covers of each of these books, and, like Szep, his work is another reason they've been enjoyed by so many people.

Matthew Carnicelli took over as editor of this series when Nancy Crossman left to strike out on her own as a literary agent. He's been everything an editor should be—patient, supportive, and understanding. More important, he's never lost his enthusiasm or his sense of humor. No small accomplishment, all things considered. Thanks to you, Matthew.

Jonathan Diamond is my agent, and he is brilliant at doing all the things that agents must do, whether they like it or not. He's supportive, but he's also very good at reining in egos that occasionally drift off into the ozone layer. As I once wrote about his predecessor, Chris Tomasino, no writer should leave home without an agent like Jonathan. Thanks again.

Thanks, too, to Bob Rosen. Bob refers to himself as the "Stepfather" of this series, and he's right. At dinner one night on the eve of the 1989 Ryder Cup Matches, Bob, as my agent in charge of all the other agents, suggested doing this book. It was a great suggestion, and I thank him for it and for his help.

Thanks as well to all the people in the game who have been so good about sharing their stories and ideas over the years. These books would not have been possible without your kind generosity.

Finally, thanks to my wife, Julia, and our three remarkable kids, Ben, Darcy, and Andy.

This one's for you, with love.

# ARCHITECTS

While golf course architects, living and dead, have become some of the most celebrated figures in the game, the truth is, many of the world's finest courses were designed by rank amateurs. Take the case of the Kawana Oshima course, some ninety miles from Tokyo, which was built in the mid-1930s.

The course's owner was a successful businessman named Kishichiro Okura, but in truth, he never set out to build a golf course. In fact, its creation came as a total surprise.

Initially, Mr. Okura wanted to develop a meadow on his large piece of property, but the man he hired to design the meadow told him that the lava subsurface of the land was ill-suited for the purpose. Instead, he suggested that Mr. Okura build a golf course on the property.

Now, golf was hardly a widely popular sport in Japan at that time. For that matter, Mr. Okura had little if any interest in the game. He dismissed the suggestion with a wave of his hand, strolled around for a while longer, and left.

Several months went by and he decided to return to check on the progress of his meadow. What he discovered was both good news and bad news.

The bad news was that, as meadows went, he had a good golf course.

1

The good news was that, as golf courses went, he had a very good one, indeed.

Mr. Okura was a little confused and more than a little miffed. He demanded an explanation.

"I started to build a meadow," he said. "But every day a golf course kept appearing, so I just let nature have her way."

The explanation was good enough for Mr. Okura, who not only okayed the completion of the course but gave the go-ahead for the construction of a second course, the Fuji, with spectacular views of Mr. Okura's beloved mountain.

# TOMMY ARMOUR

Tommy Armour, who won the U.S. and British Opens as well as a PGA Championship, enjoyed a reputation as an outstanding teacher. He was best known for the years he spent teaching at Winged Foot, but he also taught for a time at Medinah, the huge and celebrated golf mecca in the Chicago suburbs.

For all his skill as a teacher, however, Armour was far from the touchy-feely teachers we've grown so accustomed to today. For example, the mind boggles at the thought of the irascible Armour saying something as cloying as "What we want to feel in our golf swing is a sense of freedom. . . ."

And on and on.

No, Armour was one tough guy. The Scottish-born Armour had served valiantly in the British army during World War I and had been badly wounded, losing the sight of one eye to shrapnel.

While Armour was undoubtedly a fine teacher, his methods were unorthodox, to say the least. He would sit in a lawn chair under a large umbrella, usually with a gin buck resting on a table within handy reach. From there, he would issue curt instructions to the string of wealthy swells who sought him out for a miracle cure.

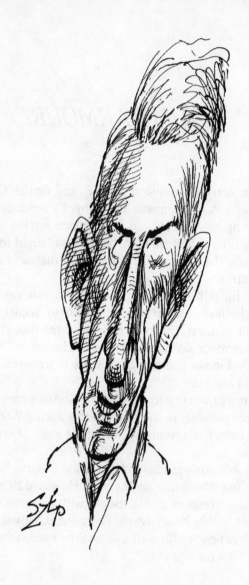

At Medinah, he also had the unnerving habit of dispatching nearby squirrels with a round from his .22 pistol. Despite his war injury, he was an excellent shot.

Still, celebrity or no celebrity, this particular habit didn't always sit well with his pupils, and finally one complained.

"Say, when are you going to take care of me?" the offended pupil complained.

"Don't tempt me," Armour said, fingering the revolver.

Armour faced down the likes of Bobby Jones, Gene Sarazen, and Walter Hagen in his playing career. After he was retired, a writer asked him whom he liked playing against.

"Rich guys with fast backswings," Armour said.

In the 1933 U.S. Open, Ralph Guldahl missed a six-foot putt on the final green at North Shore Country Club near Chicago. It would have gotten him into a playoff with Johnny Goodman—the last amateur to win the Open.

Standing near the 18th green, Armour overheard a member dismiss Guldahl as, in so many words, a "choker."

That was too much for Armour, who confronted the man and challenged him to a bet: the next day, Armour would meet the man on the 18th green after lunch to see if the man could make the same putt Guldahl had missed—double or nothing.

Armour was nothing if not a keen judge of human nature. He knew that worry about the bet would virtually guarantee that the man would have a sleepless night. And the knot in his stomach would make lunch all but indigestible.

Sure enough, the man missed the putt. In fact, it never even threatened the hole.

One reason Armour was such a brilliant teacher was that he understood just how complicated it is to make the game simple. Witness his thoughts on putting:

"All there is to putting is keeping the head steady and the face of the putter moving squarely across the line to the hole," he said. "The problem is there are at least a thousand different ways of doing these two things."

On another occasion, Armour summed up why he felt it was so difficult for people to master the game.

"It is ridiculous to think that a person with physical, temperamental, and manner-of-living limitations is able to play subpar or even par golf. He might as well expect to become a great painter or sculptor, master the violin or piano, or even become a scientific genius or a millionaire, simply by taking lessons and practicing. No, there's more to greatness than that. If there wasn't, greatness would be meaningless."

# AUGUSTA NATIONAL GOLF CLUB

Clifford Roberts is widely, and justifiably, credited with making Augusta National and the Masters the golf institutions they are today. When it came to the tournament, Roberts was a man who seldom took no for an answer.

One year he wanted to shift the tournament's dates, so it was played slightly earlier in April.

"The problem, Cliff," a committee member said, "is that means we'll finish on Easter Sunday."

"Well, who's in charge of scheduling Easter this year?" Roberts asked. "We'll get them to move it."

To his enormous credit, Clifford Roberts was a great innovator. It's no accident, for example, that the Masters is the most spectator-friendly tournament in the world.

One year, at the suggestion of CBS producer-director Frank Chirkinian, the Masters switched to scoreboards that had red numbers for players under par and green numbers for players over par.

When someone pointed out that this would not be helpful for fans who were color blind, and therefore couldn't differentiate between red and green, Roberts had a simple solution.

"That's why we have our members out there in their Green Jackets," Roberts said. "People can just ask a member for help."

Oh.

In one early Masters, a certain Count John de Bendern (formerly John de Forest, the 1932 British Amateur champion), was playing the 13th hole. His approach landed on the back of Rae's Creek, and after much study, the Count decided it was playable.

As the gallery looked on, de Bendern carefully removed his left shoe and stocking, then meticulously rolled up his left pants leg above his knee.

After more careful study, the Count moved carefully down the slope, set his right foot—shoe and all—into the water, and played the ball back onto the green.

Realizing his mistake, the Count was not amused.

The same could not be said of the gallery.

In the 1960s, a bunker was placed on the right side of the 2nd hole's landing area. It caused many players to drive the ball left, often with disastrous results, as balls bounced into the trees, shrubs, or even into the creek, which runs down the hill.

After playing the hole for the first time since the bunker was added, Gardner Dickinson was asked his opinion of the change.

"I think they ought to move the airline ticket office down there," said Dickinson. "Anyone who hit it left might as well book their flight home."

# SEVE BALLESTEROS

The reverence in which Seve Ballesteros is held in his native Spain transcends his status as a champion who has won three British Opens and two Masters and has been the heart and soul of the European Ryder Cup team. Indeed, Seve is a national hero, even a national treasure.

After he won the 1979 British Open at Royal Lytham & St. Annes, he returned home as a conquering hero. His visit to the city of Jerez prompted a series of banquets and flamenco festivals.

But the highest honor came when a 110-gallon cask of sherry was dedicated in his honor. The cask rests alongside those of . . . oh, Napoleon, Churchill, and the Beatles.

All and all, not bad company.

Seve Ballesteros's genius for shotmaking, particularly around the greens, is unchallenged. But there are times when he leaves even the most gimlet-eyed professionals shaking their heads in awe and admiration.

"I was playing with Seve one year at Augusta," remembers Raymond Floyd. "He missed the 4th green and had to come over a bunker, land the ball on the downslope, and try to keep it on the green. Not only did he pull the shot off, he actually stopped it short of the hole. I couldn't believe he even tried the shot. I dropped my club and applauded him. To this day, I tell people I was there and I saw it, but I still don't believe my eyes."

Even in his prime, Seve's driving left something to be desired. Witness the final round of the 1979 British Open at Royal Lytham and St. Annes, when he beat Ben Crenshaw and Jack Nicklaus by three strokes.

On the 16th hole, Ballesteros blew the ball way down the right side, through the rough, and into a car park some twenty-five yards wide of the fairway.

He made a birdie three, threading his second shot—a breathtaking pitch-and-run between two bunkers. Lee Trevino called it one of the greatest shots he's ever seen.

On the 18th hole, Ballesteros ripped a drive to the left side of the hole.

"What's over there?" he asked his caddie, Dave Musgrove.

"I don't know," Dave said. "It's the only place on the course we haven't been this week."

# PATTY BERG

By any standard, Patty Berg is one of the greatest players in the history of women's golf. She was one of the founding members of the Ladies Professional Golf Association and won fifty-seven tournaments.

More important than her victories, however, were her tireless efforts in promoting golf. Under the sponsorship of Wilson Sporting Goods since 1940, she traveled the country—indeed, the world—giving exhibitions. No audience was ever too small, and her enthusiasm never failed. Even into her eighties, she's capable of delivering stem-winding speeches that would do any old-time politician credit.

When World War II broke out, Patty Berg served as a lieutenant in the Marine Corps. When the war ended, she resumed her playing career and won the inaugural U.S. Women's Open Championship in 1946.

At the awards ceremony, she was handed a trophy and a check for $500. She kept the trophy but returned the money.

"Please use it to help promote junior golf," she said.

When Patty Berg was fifteen, she entered her first tournament, the Minneapolis Ladies Championship. She was placed in the last flight after shooting a 122 in the qualifying round.

Her opponent was an older woman who beat her like a drum, closing her out 10 & 8.

When she returned home and told her father how badly she'd been beaten, he tried to console her.

"Don't feel too bad, Patty," he said. "You aren't used to playing thirty-six holes. You probably got tired."

"Dad, it was just eighteen holes," said Patty.

"Oh, dear," said her father. "Did you do anything right?"

"Well, I remembered to pay my caddie," she said.

# *JOHN BLAND*

**S**outh Africa's John Bland is one of the most popular play-ers on the Senior PGA Tour and has long been a success-ful player in Europe. When he prepared to leave for the States and try his luck as a senior, his friends kidded him unmerci-fully about his chances. Finally, Bland had heard enough.

"I told them that not only would I succeed in America, but that just to prove I was incapable of bearing a grudge, I was willing to share my good fortune with them," Bland recalled.

And so he has. Every time he cashes a decent check, he sends each of his friends a crisp one-dollar bill—with his best wishes.

**O**ne of Bland's best friends is Zimbabwe's Tony Johnstone, and they have played practical jokes on each other for decades.

One night, Johnstone was having a party at his lovely house near London. Johnstone is particularly proud of the immaculately landscaped grounds, and that's where Bland went to work.

Midway through the party, Bland invited one of the guests outside for a quick golf lesson. Soon, one large divot after another was sailing across the yard, and it was only a matter of minutes before Johnstone emerged and looked in horror at his yard, which was littered with chunks of turf.

"I had stopped at a nearby golf course and filled a bag with old divots," Bland recalled. "I hid them in the bushes, and when we went out for our 'lesson,' we just hid behind the shrubs and threw the divots across the yard. I thought Tony was going to expire on the spot."

One day Bland decided to buy a new car. He went to a Ford dealership, saw a car he liked, and climbed behind the wheel. He started the car and shifted it into gear.

Wrong gear.

The car took off in reverse and smashed into the show-room wall.

"On second thought, the color's not quite right," Bland said calmly to the salesman, who looked on in disbelief, trying to figure out how he was going to explain this to the boss.

# *TOMMY BOLT*

L et's get this straight: Tommy Bolt should be in the World Golf Hall of Fame.

Not for his victory in the 1958 U.S. Open at Southern Hills.

And not for his eleven other official Tour victories or his role in helping to get the Senior Tour up and running.

No, Tommy Bolt should be in the Hall of Fame for providing more writers with more great copy than any player before or since. Old Tom, as he called himself, was—and still is—beautiful.

"O ne year Tommy was playing at Colonial and he hit a bad approach to one of the greens," Dave Marr remembered. "That was all it took. He snapped the club over his knee and sent both ends flying. Dan Jenkins wrote about it, and when Tommy read Dan's piece he took issue—and let Dan know about it. When Dan pointed out that he was right there when Tom erupted, Tommy had an answer for him.

"'It was a 5-iron, not a 4,' he said. 'Why can't you guys ever get your facts straight?'"

Like anyone else, occasionally the frustrations of a round would build up and get to be too much for Tommy Bolt.

At one tournament, the poor conditions of the greens, coupled with some uninspired play on his part, sent him over the edge. On one of the closing holes, his ball came to rest on the edge of the green, near the gallery.

As Tommy knelt behind the ball, lining up his putt, a man in the gallery kept moving from side to side, trying to get a better view. Unfortunately, his shadow kept moving back and forth over Tommy's ball.

"Could you stand still?" Bolt asked the man. "Even Old Tom can't read weeds in the dark."

# *JULIUS BOROS*

Just prior to his discharge from the U.S. Army Air Force in 1945, Julius Boros was diagnosed with a rheumatic heart condition. He asked his doctor what precautions he should take to protect his health.

"You can still play the occasional nine holes of golf every now and then, but I must warn you that you should play slow and don't take the game too seriously," the doctor said.

The first part was easy. Julius Boros never hurried in his life, either on or off the course.

As for the second part, he cheated just a bit. After joining the Tour in 1949 (forsaking the glamorous life as an accountant in Bridgeport, Connecticut), he won eighteen Tour events, including two U.S. Opens and a PGA Championship.

So much for modern medicine.

No one ever made golf look more like a stroll in the park than Julius Boros did. By comparison, even Freddie Couples looks like he's grinding out there.

With that in mind, Ben Hogan, the captain of the 1967 United States Ryder Cup team, paid Boros the ultimate compliment:

"Gentlemen," he said at a team meeting prior to the start of the matches. "When you get out there tomorrow, a hundred-piece band is going to play the national anthems, the flags will be raised, and you'll each be introduced to the crowd. I need someone who can walk to the first tee after all that and hit a long one right down the middle. I've decided to choose you, Julius. You'll probably sleep through the opening ceremony, anyway, so you'll hit the first drive for us."

Sure enough—and to no one's surprise—Boros opened the matches by striking one right into the heart of the first fairway.

In 1963, Julius Boros visited The Country Club in Brookline, Massachusetts, to play a practice round prior to the U.S. Open.

After changing into his golf shoes in the parking lot, he walked to the pro shop, where he encountered the club's long-time and legendary caddiemaster, Fred Anders, who served the club from 1940 to 1970.

Boros, a New England native who had won the 1952 U.S. Open and been named the PGA of America's Player of the Year, introduced himself to Anders and said he'd like to play the course if it wasn't too busy.

Anders assured Boros that would be fine, but he'd have to pay a greens fee just like any other guest.

Boros was dumbfounded.

Anders was insistent.

Boros refused.

Anders couldn't have cared less.

Boros walked back to his car, changed his shoes, and left.

Anders went back to caddiemastering.

Boros returned a few weeks later and won the Open, beating Arnold Palmer and Jackie Cupit in a playoff.

# *JOHNNY BULLA*

Johnny Bulla grew up in a strict Quaker family in Burlington, North Carolina. The family didn't have much money, so when the eleven-year-old learned he could make twenty-five cents a round caddying at a nearby golf course, he leapt at the chance—to the dismay of his parents.

"I'd go to church in the morning and then tell my parents I was going off to meditate in the woods," Bulla remembers. "I'd go off into the woods all right, and right to the golf course."

Soon he was hooked on the game and began playing in tournaments, often hitchhiking to the courses. This not only angered his mother, it worried her as well.

"If you play in a tournament and get killed in a car accident on Sunday when you should be at church, I'll never get over it," she told him.

"Well, if I get killed on a Monday, will you get over it?" he asked, logically enough.

As a boy, Johnny Bulla used to caddie in his bare feet—not because he couldn't afford shoes, but because it allowed him to pick balls out of deep lies in the rough and leave them in a more desirable position. Naturally, this was a skill that was widely appreciated by his golfers—whether they realized he was doing it or not.

One day one of his regular golfers was playing a local doctor in a match. On one of the closing holes, Bulla improved his player's lie, and it allowed the man to go on and win the match. Later, the doctor approached Bulla and asked the fourteen-year-old to caddie for him the following weekend in Pinehurst.

Bulla jumped at the chance, and after eighteen holes the doctor took him to a bus stop, handed him some change, and gave him a warning.

"I saw you teeing that ball up the other day," he said. "Don't ever do that again."

Johnny Bulla met Sam Snead at the 1935 Louisville Open and the two became best friends, often traveling together to tournaments in Bulla's powerful roadster.

One year, while playing in Los Angeles, they decided to go to the Rose Bowl game. Since they were running a little late, Bulla was speeding along. Soon he looked in the rearview mirror and saw the flashing lights of a police car. He started to pull to the side of the road when Sam talked him out of it.

"Let that foot get heavy," Sam said. "We've got as much speed as him and a full tank. I bet you he don't, and I don't feel like paying any speeding tickets, so let's go."

On another of their trips, they drove through Phoenix, which should in no way be confused with the Phoenix of today. It was basically a small outpost in the midst of a very large desert.

"Sambo, I'm gonna live here one day," he said.

"Are you crazy?" Sam said. "Rattlesnakes can't live here."

When they first started traveling together on tour, Bulla and Snead had a standing five-dollar bet. Whoever had the best finish that week would win five dollars from the other. It was a bet that didn't last long.

"We were playing in Los Angeles, and after I finished my round I walked out to the 18th fairway to watch Sam," Bulla remembered. "He hit a good drive, and I said to him, 'Jackson, that looks like a 6-iron to me.' He just looked at me, said 'Uh-huh,' and hit a 7-iron six feet from the hole.

"You forced it," I said.

"Pay up," he said.

"The next week he beat me again, and I told him, 'Sambo, the game's off.'"

Johnny Bulla was paired with Ralph Guldahl in the 1939 U.S. Open and was playing very well—no thanks to the gamesmanship of the man who had won both the 1937 and 1938 Opens.

"I had an eight-footer that would give me a 29, and I'll admit I was a little nervous," said Bulla. "As we got to the green, Ralph asked me 'Are you scared?' He stood real close to me as I lined up my putt, and just as I was setting up over the ball, he said, 'John, are you sure you know how this is going to break?'"

Not surprisingly, Bulla missed the putt. And not surprisingly, he didn't hang on to win the Open, either.

# CADDIES

In the 1928 British Open at Royal St. Georges, Gene Sarazen had a caddie named Skip Daniels. The two men were very fond of each other, but as the championship progressed it was clear that something was wrong with Daniels.

"I started out pretty well, but as the tournament went on, my play got worse and worse," Sarazen remembered. "Skip kept saying, 'Oh, you're hitting the ball so well, sir.' I couldn't figure out what was going on, until I learned he'd been gassed in World War I and it was causing his vision to go bad."

During the 1999 Ryder Cup at The Country Club in Brookline, Massachusetts, a writer took some time off to play at one of the local clubs.

In the course of the round, one member of the foursome mentioned that he'd been having a problem sleeping. His caddie offered a solution.

"I had that problem myself, and one of the members suggested that when I go to bed at night, I try to play a round of

golf in my mind," the caddie said. "He told me it would help me relax and fall asleep."

The golfer asked the caddie if it worked.

"Oh, it worked like a charm for a while," he said. "But then I drove it into the woods on the 6th hole, spent twenty minutes looking for the ball, and got so upset that I was up all night."

In 1935, a promising young amateur named Ray Billows traveled to Winged Foot Golf Club outside New York City for the New York State Amateur. He was strapped for cash—the Model T Ford he'd bought for fifteen dollars barely made it to the course—and when he got to the first tee, tournament officials informed him that he had to take a caddie. Billows protested, but the officials were insistent. No caddie, no golf.

As luck would have it, a kid in the gallery overheard the discussion, picked up Billows's bag, and followed him off the tee and down the fairway.

"Look, I can't afford to pay you," Billows said to the boy.

"I don't care," the caddie said. "No one's forcing me. I want to do it. I think you can win."

Sure enough, at the end of thirty-six holes, Billows was tied with a talented player named Jack Creavy and went on to beat him on the first hole of sudden death.

A few years later, with a few dollars more to his credit, Billows returned to Winged Foot, found the caddie, and handed him $100—for his efforts and for his confidence.

Billows, by the way, went on to win seven state amateur titles and lost in the finals of the U.S. Amateur three times.

Still, one of his greatest thrills came in a casual match with Bobby Jones in 1939 at Augusta National.

He won a dollar in the match and asked Jones to pay him by check. Billows had the check framed.

More than sixty years later, the check still hangs on a wall in his home.

In the final round of the 1960 Masters, Arnold Palmer found himself locked in a battle with Ken Venturi. The pressure mounted on the back nine, and when Palmer hit a poor chip on the 15th hole, he lost his temper and tossed his club to his caddie, Ironman.

Ironman glared at Palmer.

"Boss, are we chokin'?" he asked.

"Par, birdie, birdie," answered Palmer, who went on to win his second Masters by a single stroke over Venturi.

Craig Stadler traveled to St. Andrews as part of the winning 1975 American Walker Cup team. Along with many of his teammates, he traveled to Hoylake for the British Amateur Championship.

When Stadler arrived at Hoylake, he was assigned a caddy named Jimmy Scouse. It was not a marriage made in heaven.

Scouse could be difficult, to say the least, and didn't harbor any particular love for Americans. For his part, let's just say Stadler can also be strong-willed, to put it mildly.

It wasn't long before the two got into an argument. It quickly escalated until Scouse picked up Stadler's bag, threw it at him, and stormed off to the nearest pub.

He did not return to get paid.

# JOANNE GUNDERSON CARNER

By any standard, JoAnne Gunderson Carner is one of the greatest players in golf history, and also one of the most beloved.

Just consider her record: She is the only player to win the USGA's Girls' and Amateur championships as well as the Women's Open. She won the Girls' and Women's Amateur in consecutive years. She won five Women's Amateur titles and two U.S. Women's Opens, and her total of eight USGA national championships ties her with Jack Nicklaus—one back of Bob Jones—as the winner of the greatest number of USGA championships. A member of the LPGA's Hall of Fame, she won forty-two tour events, including the 1969 Burdine's Invitational in Miami—the last time an amateur won an LPGA event.

Unlike many players of her era, "The Great Gundy," as she was known, didn't come from a country club background. Instead, she learned the game on the fine public courses of her native Seattle. Girls didn't caddie in those days, but Gundy found a way to make a few bucks from the game. She shagged balls for players while they practiced, tended the flowers and shrubs, and, more lucratively, hunted for golf balls with her brother.

The used-ball business came to an end one day when the owner of the nine-hole Juanita Golf Club caught the sixteen-year-old searching for balls in the underbrush alongside a pond.

"I moved, and one of the people in his foursome heard the leaves rustle," Carner said. She said, 'There's a deer or something in there,' and she started down toward the shrubs. I figured the jig was up, so I walked out.

"'That's not a deer,' the owner said. 'That's the state champion.'"

Carner excelled at match play—witness her amateur record—but in truth she was even more dominating than the record shows.

"One night we were talking over drinks, and I said I thought you had to have a real killer instinct to be successful at match play, much more so than medal play," remembered Carner's late friend and teacher, Gardner Dickinson. "I told her that when I played Ryder Cup, if I had a guy 3-down I couldn't wait to get him 4-down. I might be the guy's best friend off the course, but once we teed it up, I wanted to grind him into the ground. JoAnne told me that when she got somebody she knew she could beat down early in a match, she'd let them back in the game, then come back and beat them. From that point on, I always figured that the secret to her success was that she played the game for the sheer joy of it—and humiliating another player would take some of the joy out of the game for her."

# *HENRY COTTON*

In the 1920s, professional golfers in Great Britain and Ireland were treated as glorified caddies—if they were even accorded that much stature. Naturally, this grated on someone with Henry Cotton's considerable sense of self.

One day Cotton, who would win the 1934, '37, and '48 British Opens, traveled to Portmarnock, north of Dublin, for an exhibition. Cotton won the match, and the members applauded enthusiastically, thanked Cotton for his efforts, and then repaired to the clubhouse—where neither Cotton nor any of his fellow professionals were allowed.

Undeterred, Cotton made his way to the parking lot, where he sat in his elegant Bentley limousine and was served an elaborate lunch by his white-gloved butler.

Looking at today's professional golfers, with their dedication to health and fitness, it's easy to forget that for most of this century the top players were known to take a drink. Or two. Or more, for that matter.

This made the elegant Cotton something of an exception. For much of his career—and certainly in his younger days—he rarely, if ever, let alcohol pass his lips. This was the case in 1929, when he was a member of the Great Britain/Ireland Ryder Cup team.

The matches were played at Moortown Golf Club in Leeds, West Yorkshire, and each evening Cotton and his teammates would gather in the bar of their hotel, the Majestic. It was decided, in advance, that at the end of the evening the bills would be divided equally among the team members.

When the first round was ordered, Cotton asked the bartender if the hotel had any Comice pears, a particular favorite of Cotton's. Naturally, the thought of anyone standing around in a bar eating pears when they could be tossing back perfectly good scotch struck the pros as comical bordering on the bizarre.

But they didn't think it was quite so funny when the bill came and they discovered that Cotton's beloved pears—which were out of season—were more expensive than even the finest whiskey.

Whatever their consternation, the boys got over it, rallying to beat the Yanks, 7–5, for their first Ryder Cup victory.

# DEAR OLD DAD

After losing to Nick Faldo in a playoff for the 1989 Masters, a dejected Scott Hoch returned to the clubhouse with his family. As he entered the locker room, he slapped the top of the doorjamb.

"What happened, Daddy?" asked his five-year-old son, Cameron.

"I messed up," Hoch said.

"Again?" Cameron asked.

Chi Chi Rodriguez's first PGA victory came at the 1963 Denver Open, but it was a victory tinged with a note of sadness.

"I was paired with Ken Still, and during the round I saw a man approaching us from about six hundred yards away," Rodriguez remembered. "I've always had this ability to see into the future—to know when something was going to happen—I knew when I saw the man that he had a telegram telling me that my father had died. As he got closer, he called to me and told me he had something for me. I said to Ken, 'I know, it's a telegram. My father is dead.' Sure enough, that's exactly what happened. I left right away and went home to Puerto Rico."

# JIMMY DEMARET

On a visit to Barcelona for a match in the old "Shell's Wonderful World of Golf" series, local officials arranged an audience with the Cardinal of Barcelona for Jimmy Demaret, Gene Sarazen, and the series' producer and director, Fred Raphael.

After the formalities, the Cardinal offered a blessing and closed by making the sign of the cross.

"In the name of the Father," he said, looking at Sarazen, the oldest of the three.

"And of the Son," he said, looking at Raphael, the youngest of the three.

"And of the Holy Spirit," he said, looking at Demaret, who was easily the most spirited of the bunch.

Jimmy Demaret and Bob Hope were good friends. One day Hope asked Demaret the question that's on every hacker's

lips: "Jimmy, with my game, what do I have to do to be a consistent winner?"

"Cheat," said Demaret without missing a beat.

Here's Jimmy Demaret on:

His early days on tour: "We didn't have money, but we did have an Oklahoma credit card—a siphon hose."

A fellow player's drinking habits: "I wouldn't say he's a drunk, but he can outdrink Dean Martin with one lip tied behind his back."

His favorite drink: "The next one."

The Bible: "The Bible teaches 'an eye for an eye, a tooth for a tooth.' I think that's a little harsh. I believe in a joke for a joke."

Jimmy Demaret always claimed he got his sense of style from his father.

"My daddy had a wonderful sense of mixing and matching colors," Demaret once told a writer.

"Was your father in the clothing business?" the writer asked.

"No, he was a housepainter," Demaret said, laughing. "But he was the Michelangelo of housepainters."

Jimmy Demaret loved to party, and one of his favorite companions was singer Phil Harris. One year at a tournament, Demaret finished his third round and a writer asked him how he played.

"I made 10 the hard way," he said. "I was out with Phil 'til five in the morning two nights in a row."

In one of his last visits to the Masters, a writer asked Jimmy Demaret if he thought the game was better than when he was playing.

"Oh, much better," said Demaret. "When I won my last Masters, I got $800. Now they pay me $1,000 just to show up for dinner."

One day a writer, who was perhaps taking himself and golf a little too seriously, asked Jimmy Demaret if he thought golf was like life.

"I'm not sure," Demaret said. "Except that the older you get the harder it is to score."

In 1968, Sam Snead played Roberto de Vicenzo at Congressional Country Club in a "Shell's Wonderful World of Golf" match. It was about this time that Sam began to have problems with his putting and began experimenting with different styles. He finally settled on an effective—if ungainly—method; he'd putt with the ball between his feet and his hands set widely apart on the club. It was, for all intents and purposes, a croquet stroke.

At Congressional, Gene Sarazen had seen Sam using the stroke on the practice green, so when the match reached the first hole, he tipped off the viewers and his fellow announcer:

"Be prepared to see a new style of putting," Sarazen said.

Demaret watched Sam stroke the putt.

"He looks like a land crab," Demaret quipped.

A few holes later, Demaret had changed his mind.

"Sam looks like he's basting a turkey," Demaret said.

Make no mistake about it: for all his kidding around, Jimmy Demaret was a very tough competitor. After all, no one wins three Masters without having a certain fire burning from within. But he also had a very compassionate side to him, as the late Dave Marr once recalled.

"Jimmy finished the 1957 U.S. Open at Inverness at 283," Marr said. "He and I were in the locker room watching Dick Mayer play the 18th hole. Now, Jimmy was forty-seven at the time, so this was probably his last realistic chance to win the Open. Mayer had a putt to take the lead, and when he made it Jimmy said, 'I'm glad he made that putt. That young man really needs the money.' He really meant it, too. There was no one else around, and he certainly didn't have to try and impress me. That kind of epitomized the kind of guy Jimmy was."

# *ROBERTO DE VICENZO*

During a 1968 "Shell's Wonderful World of Golf" match with Sam Snead at Congressional, de Vicenzo birdied an especially difficult 450-yard par 4. After he putted out, Jimmy Demaret and Gene Sarazen congratulated him.

"Yes, this is a very difficult hole," de Vicenzo said. "In my country we have a name for holes like this: a par 5."

In another Shell match, one of de Vicenzo's drives hit one of the camera trucks that was camouflaged with leaves and branches. As the truck began to head down the fairway, members of the crew shouted for it to stop.

"Let it go," Roberto said. "I need a 450-yard drive on this hole."

# DISASTERS

By anyone's standards, Paul Runyan has been one of the game's greatest and most tenacious champions. Never a long hitter by any stretch of the imagination, he made up for his lack of power with an astonishing short game that allowed him to win more than fifty professional tournaments, including two PGA Championships. He was the Tour's leading money winner in 1933 and 1934.

Given all that, he figured to be a mainstay of the 1933 American Ryder Cup team at Southport & Ainsdale Golf Club. In the second day's 36-hole singles matches, he faced Percy Alliss.

The Runyan–Alliss match went out late. Ahead of them, Gene Sarazen, Walter Hagen, and Craig Wood were all winning, but Olin Dutra was on his way to a 9 & 8 pounding by Abe Mitchell. Mitchell was the professional who taught Samuel Ryder—the patron of the Ryder Cup—how to play and, for his efforts, got his likeness atop the Ryder Cup trophy.

Runyan struggled early in the match but managed to get back to even on the 34th hole.

That's when disaster struck.

On the 35th hole, both Runyan and Alliss hit their approaches into a bunker guarding the green. When they reached the green, they saw that both balls were touching, just inside the back edge of the bunker. Since Runyan was away by a matter of inches, he had the poor luck to play first.

Runyan was one of the game's finest bunker players, in no small part because he was also one of the game's finest putters as well. But the bunkers at Southport & Ainsdale were far from consistent, and given his lie, Runyan couldn't take a stance and get a feel for the texture of the sand.

Runyan's shot came out running, and for a time it looked as though it might check up and stay on the green. Instead, it rolled slowly off the edge of the green, then gained speed and ran past the 18th tee and out-of-bounds.

The usually unflappable Runyan was shocked and couldn't recover. He lost the home hole and the match. When Denny Shute three-putted the last hole and lost, 1-down, to Syd Easterbrook, the Americans had suffered a 6½–5½ defeat— their last defeat for another twenty-four years.

"That loss to Percy Boomer was one of the toughest in my career," Runyan later admitted. "I've never gotten over it."

This may not qualify as a disaster, in the strict golfing sense, but it does count as a major embarrassment.

In 1997, writer Charles Pierce was at the Mercedes Championships in La Costa working on a story. What he witnessed was a textbook case of marketing guys run amok.

"They had put these beautiful new Mercedes all over the course, so naturally people in the gallery did what people instinctively do when they look at a new car: they kicked the tires and tried to open the doors for a better look at the inside," Pierce recalls. "The only problem was that the cars were locked and had these alarm systems that went off whenever anyone tried to open the door. So every time you turned around, alarms were going off in the middle of backswings and when guys were getting ready to putt. It was a nightmare."

# FOREIGN AFFAIRS

The early 1960s was a time of political estrangement between the United States and Burma. At one point, three years passed without an American being officially invited to visit the country.

But as luck would have it, the country's president was an avid golfer, and when the State Department learned that Gene Sarazen was going to be in the region, they requested that Sarazen change his plans and fly to Rangoon for a round with the president.

At first, Sarazen declined, citing a demanding schedule. It took a call from Secretary of State Dean Rusk to change his mind—something not easily done even under the best of circumstances.

When Sarazen arrived at the stiflingly hot airport, he was met by a cadre of local hoi polloi, who escorted Sarazen and his party to the airport terminal's lounge, where the Great Man was toasted with rounds of drinks. After what seemed like hours in the insufferable heat and speeches, it came Sarazen's time to speak. Everything ran smoothly enough until the feisty Sarazen warmed to his subject and became positively Trumanesque.

"I'm told we're the first Americans you've invited here in three years," the Squire said. "Well, what the hell is wrong with you? Are you a bunch of Communists?"

Beautiful.

One year the Wilson Sporting Goods Company, which Sarazen represented for most of his career, sent him to Japan to help convince golf professionals to buy up the overstock of aluminum-shafted clubs that were filling Wilson's warehouses.

Sarazen was successful, but when he returned to Japan a year later, he found that aluminum shafts weren't any more popular in Japan than they had been in the States.

"You say aluminum shafts here to stay," one Japanese professional told Sarazen. "You right. Nobody buy. Aluminum shafts sure to stay—in pro shop."

King Hassan II of Morocco had a nine-hole course built on the grounds of his palace, and by all accounts it was a lovely little course—except for one small problem. The bunkers proved to be a bit much for His Royal Highness.

The king spared no expense in trying to improve. He regularly flew Claude Harmon, the 1948 Masters champion and longtime professional at Winged Foot and Seminole, halfway around the world for lessons. Harmon was one of the greatest bunker players in history, but even he couldn't help the king.

After years of frustration, the king issued a royal edict: he ordered every one of the fifty bunkers filled in and sodded over.

In 1950, Argentina's Roberto de Vicenzo received his first invitation to play in the Masters Tournament. Unfortunately, something was lost in the translation.

Literally.

When his reply was received at Augusta National, it read that he was delighted to accept the invitation to play in "the Annual Teachers Competition."

Back in the early days of the Royal Hong Kong Golf Club, golf was a considerably more elegant affair than it is today.

Members and their guests would ride in the club's specially appointed Pullman car from the city out to the club. During the trip out, an elaborate breakfast would be served, and once the train—the "Taipo Belle"—reached the club, rickshaws would carry golfers to the clubhouse.

Ah, for the days of Empire.

# WALTER HAGEN

The Great Haig was a true believer in the old saying "It's not how, but how many." He was once asked to describe how he made a par 4 on a hole, and he said, "One of those, one of these, and two of them makes four."

Simple enough, and so was his solution to playing the treacherous 7th hole at the famed Pebble Beach Golf Links.

Now, going just by the scorecard, the 7th should be a piece of cake. It's only 107 yards long, and since it plays straight downhill, it plays even shorter than the yardage. But as is so often the case, the numbers lie. The truth rides in on the winds, which blow off the water.

On a calm day, players can easily hit the green with a sand wedge, but when the wind is into a player's face, it may take a long iron to get home—and that's an extremely dangerous play to such a small target.

Hagen faced just those conditions during an exhibition match in the 1930s. After watching his playing companions knock ball after ball into oblivion, Hagen swallowed his pride, pulled out his putter, and ran the ball down the hill. It came to rest just short of the green, where he got up and down in two for par.

It was pure Hagen.

51

Hagen was one of the first true worldwide golf celebrities. Like most players of his era, he realized that the money he won in tournaments paled in comparison to the money he could make playing exhibitions.

On one trip through Asia, he decided to be fitted for a custom-made suit. He arranged for the tailor to come to his room late one afternoon, following a luncheon in his honor.

As luck would have it, the luncheon ran longer than Hagen had planned, and the liquor was better—or at least stronger—than he had expected. One shooter led to another, and when he returned to his room he decided to lie down and take a brief nap—which lasted for several hours.

He naturally assumed that the tailor had arrived and, finding the snoozing Haig, had quietly left. But a few days later, as he was about to leave, the suit was delivered to his hotel.

"How's the suit?" asked his friend, the trick-shot artist Joe Kirkwood.

"It's beautiful, but it only fits right when I'm lying down," Hagen said. "I guess I'll save it for my funeral."

Walter Hagen had an eye for the ladies. What he didn't have was a particularly good memory for names.

"One time I asked him, 'Walter, how do you remember all their names?'" Gene Sarazen remembered. "He said, 'Here's my secret. I just say, How you doin', sugar?' It saves me a lot of thinking, and they're just as happy.'"

Walter Hagen was known to take a drink, but in truth, reports of his drinking were greatly exaggerated—even if he did much of the exaggerating.

At the 1931 Ryder Cup Matches at Scioto Country Club in Columbus, Ohio, Hagen strolled to the first tee in his match with England's Charles Whitcomb.

With Whitcomb and the large gallery looking on, Hagen downed a glass of what he claimed was whiskey.

"A little something to calm the nerves," Hagen said to the gallery.

If Whitcomb ever had much of a chance, Hagen's gamesmanship probably did him in.

The Haig laced his opening drive deep down the fairway, and won the match, 4 & 3.

Hagen's penchant for making—and spending—money was a big part of his legend. Indeed, his earnings from exhibitions and endorsements were all but unprecedented in his time. Naturally, Hagen being Hagen, his earnings were exceeded only by his expenses.

The late Charlie Price, a gifted writer who knew Hagen well, once summed up Hagen's finances this way:

"In his prime, Hagen made more money than Babe Ruth. But, of course, he also spent more than the entire Yankee outfield."

# *BEN HOGAN*

In the last years of his career, Ben Hogan—who had been a phenomenal putter—was a basket case on the greens. And no one knew it better than he did.

After a round where he hit every fairway and every green in regulation, a fan congratulated him on his remarkable accuracy.

"I don't have any choice," said Hogan sternly. "Unlike some of these guys out here, if I miss, I lose . . . and I'm not out here to lose."

It is a testimony to the affection and respect the fans had for Hogan that in the latter years of his career, people would flock to the practice tee just to watch Hogan hit balls. When he finished and began to walk off the tee, he'd receive standing ovations.

The 1960 U.S. Open at Cherry Hills in Denver was notable for any number of reasons.

For starters, Arnold Palmer shot his dramatic, final-round 65 to win his only U.S. Open.

But for golf historians, Ben Hogan—remarkably, in contention in the Open at age forty-eight—was paired with a twenty-year-old amateur, Jack Nicklaus.

At the close of the tournament, in which Nicklaus finished second, two strokes back, Hogan famously remarked that "I played with a kid today who should have won the Open by 10 shots."

Nicklaus, in a tribute to Hogan's still-considerable ball-striking skills, responded that "if I had putted for Ben, he'd have won by 10."

Like most players of his era, Hogan played by sight, not yardage.

But toward the end of his career, yardage books were becoming popular—not that Hogan had much faith in them.

Hogan had a habit of standing behind the ball, visualizing the shot he wanted to play. On one occasion his caddie—who was either very brave, very confident, or very dense—offered a little helpful information to Hogan as he pondered his next shot.

"It's 146, 147 yards to the pin, Mr. Hogan," the caddie said.

"Make up your mind, son," said Hogan.

In 1953, Ben Hogan traveled to Carnoustie, Scotland, for his only appearance in the British Open. He arrived two weeks before the championship to familiarize himself with both the golf course and the small British ball. It is also worth noting that, even though he was Ben Hogan—which should have been enough in and of itself—as well as the reigning Masters and U.S. Open champion, he still had to play in a qualifying event.

Carnoustie was unlike any course Hogan had ever seen, but through his tenacious practice, he came to understand and appreciate it. What baffled him, however, was that the trajectory of his shots began to vary widely. This was particularly troublesome for Hogan, who believed that achieving consistent trajectory was a key to solid shotmaking.

At first, Hogan thought the problem might be the small ball, but upon close examination of his irons, he realized that the ground was so hard that it was altering the loft of his clubs, forcing him to check them after each round.

Hogan captained the United States Ryder Cup team that traveled to Glanton Golf Club in Scarborough, England, for the 1949 matches.

At the time, Great Britain—all of Europe, actually—was still reeling from the effects of World War II. Rations were a particular problem, so Hogan arranged for a wide variety of meats and produce—in enormous quantities—to be shipped over on the Queen Mary when the team made its Atlantic crossing.

The Americans graciously hosted the Great Britain/Ireland team to a pretournament dinner, but that failed to satisfy the

British newspapers, which fueled the fires of resentment among their readers. Finally, Hogan had heard enough.

"We came over here to play golf, not talk about meat," Hogan told the writers. "If the British public is so interested in meat, we'll come over next time and put on a meat exhibition instead of a golf match."

A writer once asked Nick Price, a native of Zimbabwe, if Ben Hogan had been an influence on his career. Price smiled, reached into his golf bag, and pulled out a small sequence of Hogan's swing.

"Not at all," Price said. "I only look at this four or five times a week."

B en Hogan was a man of few words, to put it mildly. But like so many other parts of his life, there was a certain irrefutable logic to his silence.

"People who talk all the time never learn anything," Hogan once told a friend. "There's another advantage to choosing your words carefully: if you keep quiet, people may suspect you're not very smart, but it will be harder for them to prove it."

Part of the considerable Hogan legend stems from his relentless pursuit of perfection, which included his "Secret," which eventually led to his powerful, reliable, and repeatable swing. It was a pursuit that took longer than most people realized.

"I had met Byron Nelson when we were paired together in the 1955 Thunderbird tournament in Palm Springs," recalled John Jacobs, the widely respected British player and teacher. "I didn't see him again until the 1967 [British] Open Championship at Hoylake. We sat and had a lovely conversation, and after a time I asked him about his friend Ben Hogan and his career.

"It's a funny thing about Ben that most people don't realize," Byron said. "It was a grip change that was really the reason he got so good. It prevented him from hitting a hook unless he wanted to. But it took Ben a good three years before he trusted it. He'd practice and practice with that grip, but when he got to the first tee he'd go back to the old grip and those hooks would appear. Once he got so he trusted the change, then he started winning the way people remember him today."

Ben Hogan had a keen, analytical mind, and he applied that intelligence to his pursuit of excellence.

"At one point, Ben noticed that late in a round he'd have trouble hitting his 4-wood just the way he wanted," his protégé, the late Gardner Dickinson, once recalled. "To figure out why, he waited until the end of his practice sessions, when

59

he'd be tired, to work on his fairway woods. That's just how meticulous Ben was."

To say that Ben Hogan's standards were exacting is to put it mildly.

"Sometimes I'd go over to Colonial to watch Ben practice," recalls the great writer Dan Jenkins. "Sometimes he'd invite me out to play and he'd go around Colonial from the back tees and shoot a 66, 67, or 68 and make it look easy. One time, after we played we went in for a drink and I told him, 'Ben, that's as good a round as I've ever seen.' He said, 'No it wasn't. I only hit about two shots the way I wanted to.'"

Ben Hogan existed in the rarefied air of the greatest champions. But in expressing his feelings for golf, he spoke for everyone who loves the game.

"The prospect that there was going to be golf in my day made me feel privileged and happy, and I couldn't wait for the sun to come up the next morning so that I could get out on the course again."

# *MARION HOLLINS*

D r. Alister Mackenzie is generally credited with designing Cypress Point Golf Club in Monterey, California, but in truth, much of the credit should be shared with Marion Hollins. In fact, in many reports of the day, she is credited with being the club's founder.

The initial routing for the course was done by Seth Raynor, but he died before construction could begin. In Raynor's design, the 231-yard 16th hole was planned as a dogleg par 4 with a tee shot across an inlet that required a carry of some 200 yards. When Mackenzie visited the site, he agreed with Raynor's design.

But Hollins, a fine player who won the 1921 U.S. Women's Amateur, disagreed and argued that the hole would be better as a par 3. In fact, she said, it would be one of the greatest par 3s in the world. When Mackenzie and the other men argued that it was an impossible carry, Hollins pulled out a 2-wood and ripped the ball over the water, onto the point of land where the green sits today.

End of discussion.

Marion Hollins won the 1941 women's championship at Cypress Point, on a day when the weather was quite simply awful. The rain came down in sheets, and Hollins had to regularly stop and ring out the two cashmere sweaters she was wearing to ward off the cold.

Of the forty players who started the day, all but four quit and walked in. Even Hollins had her reservations. At one point she looked at her dog, Ganz, who always followed her on the course. Seeing a workman nearby, she asked him to take the dog back to the clubhouse.

"This is no kind of weather for a dog to be out in," she said.

In the end, Hollins shot a remarkable 91 on a day when no one else even broke 100.

# JOHN JACOBS

John Jacobs is one of the finest players produced by England in the post–World War II era, but he is perhaps best known as a teacher of both weekend players in his popular schools, and many top professionals and amateurs.

One of the players he has worked with over the years is the five-time British Open champion Peter Thomson. This anecdote speaks volumes about both Jacobs's philosophy of teaching and the brilliant simplicity of Thomson's approach to the game.

"Many years ago, Peter lived in London and I was teaching and living about twenty miles outside the city," Jacobs recalled. "Peter rang me up one day and asked if he might come out and have me look at his swing. Naturally, I told him to come right along, and after a bit he arrived, a club tucked under his arm.

"After a time, he took his address position and asked me how it looked.

"'Perfect,' I said.

"'Thanks very much, then,' Peter said.

"With that, he drove off without hitting even so much as one ball, satisfied that he was quite prepared for the Open Championship."

Beyond his skill as a golfer, John Jacobs is an accomplished fisherman—and one day that skill paid off handsomely.

In 1978, Jacobs was fishing on the river Avon in Dorset. As luck—or skill—would have it, he landed a twenty-seven-pound salmon, which he sold to a local hotel for £130.

One day, in the course of an interview, Jacobs found himself being praised effusively for his playing skills.

"Thank you," Jacobs said. "You know, it's a funny thing, but the older I get, the better I used to be."

# BOBBY JONES

Bobby Jones was not only a supreme champion but also a magnificent sportsman. Still, that's not to say that he didn't have a formidable temper, not only in his early years but even in casual rounds after his championship career was over.

"In truth," he once wrote, "golf is sometimes a game that cannot be endured with a club in my hands."

Johnny Bulla remembers just how intense Jones could be, even years after he retired from tournament golf.

"I used to play a fair amount with Bob at East Lake in the years after he quit playing in championships," Bulla recalls. "One time we came to the last hole all even and Bob three-putted to lose our match. We went to the locker room, and Bob sat down, took off one of his shoes, and threw it at his locker. We played a few weeks later, and Bob three-putted the last hole to lose. I didn't go to the locker room this time."

Bob Jones was very close to his father, whom everyone referred to as "the Colonel."

The Colonel was a passionate, if average, golfer, but he was one of his famous son's favorite playing companions.

When Augusta National was first built, Jones and architect Dr. Alister Mackenzie had a pot bunker placed in the middle of the 11th fairway, where it wasn't visible from the tee.

In his first round at Augusta National, the Colonel hit his drive into the bunker. When he reached his ball, he let out a dazzling string of expletives, for which he was famous.

"Who was the goddamned idiot who put that goddamned bunker in the middle of this goddamned fairway?" he bellowed.

"I did," his son replied, laughing.

While the U.S. Amateur holds a special place in the hearts of golf purists, in truth, it's long been overshadowed by the four professional major championships. But back in the 1920s and early '30s, when Bob Jones dominated golf, the Amateur was as important as any championship in the world.

In 1929, the U.S. Amateur came west of the Mississippi for the first time. It was played at Del Monte Country Club (Pebble Beach Golf Links), and Jones was the defending champion and prohibitive favorite. In fact, some people believe that the heavy betting in the Calcutta may have led to Jones's upset loss at the hands of Johnny Goodman.

According to legend, a millionaire named Henry Lapham bought Jones for $23,000 and hedged his bet by getting Francis Ouimet, the 1913 U.S. Open and 1914 (and 1931) U.S. Amateur champion, for $8,000.

Burdened with the added pressure, Jones faced Goodman—a relative unknown who hopped a freight train to get to California. Goodman was, in fact, a talented golfer who would go on to win the 1937 Amateur and, in 1933, become the last amateur to win the U.S. Open.

Jones bogeyed the 14th to fall, 1-down, to Goodman. His putt for a birdie and a win on 17 hung on the lip and seemed to take the fight out of the great champion. The two men halved the 18th and the match was over.

Jones spent the rest of the week admiring the work of architect Alister Mackenzie at nearby Cypress Point. He was so taken by Mackenzie's design that, a few years later, he hired him to design Augusta National.

Harrison R. Johnston went on to beat one Dr. O. F. Willing in the finals—before a small gallery. Fully half the fans lost interest after Jones was defeated and never returned to the course.

By 1926, Bobby Jones and Walter Hagen were arguably the two best golfers in the world.

Hagen had already won the PGA Championship in 1921, '24, '25, and '26 and would go on to win the championship in 1927 as well. In addition, he'd already won two British Opens and two U.S. Opens.

For his part, by the end of 1926, Jones had won two U.S. Opens, a British Open, and two U.S. Amateurs.

So naturally, when Jones and Hagen agreed to play a seventy-two-hole exhibition match, newspapers across the United States and Great Britain trumpeted the story in one article after another.

Alas, the match turned out to be a bust. Hagen cruised to a 12 & 11 victory.

"Hagen went around the course in 71 strokes," one writer observed. "Bobby went around in 75 cigarettes."

True to character, Jones made no excuses. He did, however, make this observation:

"Exhibitions are one thing," he said. "Championships are something quite different."

Jones would go on to win eight more in the next four years, bringing his total to thirteen before he retired from competition at age twenty-eight.

As long as there are golfers, there will be a debate over who was the greatest player of all time. But at the time of his retirement from competitive play, there was no doubt how his contemporaries viewed Bobby Jones's place in history.

"I now come with faltering pen to write about the greatest of them all," wrote the legendary British golf writer Bernard Darwin.

# *BERNHARD LANGER*

To say that Bernhard Langer is an unlikely success story is to put it mildly.

That he would grow up to become a golfer, let alone the winner of two Masters Tournaments and countless tournaments around the world, is nothing short of amazing.

Langer grew up in Anhausen, Germany. Golf was an elitist sport in Germany and received virtually no press coverage. Still, Langer was intrigued by the game and was determined to become a professional.

One day, as a teenager, he went to the local employment-counseling center for advice on a golf career. The bureaucrat studiously went through all the available information and reported back that there was no record that golf was either a profession or a trade.

Undeterred, Langer went to work in the pro shop at a local country club. He tried to pattern his swing after Jack Nicklaus's, because it was the only sequence mounted on the pro shop's walls.

There's an utterly logical reason why Langer's swing turned out to be somewhat flat rather than upright like the Nicklaus model.

"The room I worked in had very low ceilings, which made it impossible for me to swing like Jack," Langer explains.

Oh well, something on the Hogan-Player variety has worked out just fine.

In the 1991 Ryder Cup matches at Kiawah Island, Langer came to the final hole on the last day, locked in a dramatic duel with Hale Irwin. In the end, the matches came down to Langer's twisting ten-footer. The pressure was so great that Irwin, as ferocious a competitor as there is, was visibly shaking as he watched Langer.

"I felt terrible for Bernhard," Jack Nicklaus said later. "No one should ever face that much pressure."

Langer's putt slid past the hole. The Americans had won, and broke into a wild celebration. Langer and the Europeans repaired to their locker room. There, Seve Ballesteros—who had frequently battled with Langer—rushed to the German's side and embraced him, tears pouring from his eyes.

"I felt I had let everyone down," Langer said later. "Seve looked me right in the eye and told me that was nonsense. I will always remember that."

# *LAW AND ORDER*

The members of The Country Club, in the Boston suburb of Brookline, are pillars of the community and, it's safe to assume, always have been. So you can imagine the reaction when, in 1895, police swept onto the club grounds and arrested thirty-three members.

It's not as bad as it sounds.

It seems that a large number of people—members and nonmembers alike—were appalled by the introduction of this odd Scottish game, golf, to quaint and sedate Brookline. Beyond that, some were horrified that people would participate in this abomination on the Sabbath, in violation of the Commonwealth's notorious "Blue Laws."

So on this fateful Sunday, a neighbor (and nonmember, mercifully) complained to the police and the joint was raided.

As luck would have it, the neighbor died before the case could go to court (well, at least it was lucky for the "Brookline 33") and the case was dropped. Not long afterward, the state legislature came to its senses and liberalized the laws, allowing golf on Sundays.

73

Back in 1967, the Ryder Cup wasn't the intense, micro-managed extravaganza it is today. Everyone understood that, barring an act of God, the United States would win, everyone would congratulate themselves on the sportsmanship of it all, and they'd meet two years later and pretty much go through the same routine.

And so it was that at the 1967 matches at Champions Golf Club in Houston, Arnold Palmer decided to break up the monotony by taking some of the Great Britain/Ireland team up for a flight in his Jet Commander.

So off they went, made a couple passes over the course highlighted by a loop-de-loop or two, and headed back to the hangar. A good time was had by all.

Well, not everyone. When they got to the hangar, they learned that several residents had called to complain that Palmer's plane had flown below the tree line and that a full-blown investigation was under way.

For their part, Palmer and his passengers insisted that the plane was never lower than 1,000 feet as it flew over the course. Still, for six weeks the FAA investigators looked into the complaint, finally throwing up their hands in the face of reams of contradictory evidence.

# HENRY LONGHURST

The late Henry Longhurst enjoyed a long and distinguished career as a golf writer and commentator. His writing appeared around the world, and he worked, at one time or another, for the BBC, CBS, and ABC.

He made his CBS debut at a tournament played at Pleasant Valley Country Club in Massachusetts. As the fates would have it, play was delayed by torrential rains, leaving Longhurst with time on his hands and wet clothing on his back. Finally, he'd had enough and called to producer/director Frank Chirkinian on his microphone.

"I say, Frank," he said. "Do you suppose I might go to the clubhouse and get as wet on the inside as I am on the outside?"

# NANCY LOPEZ

Nancy Lopez grew up in a close-knit family in Roswell, New Mexico. She learned to play golf from her father, Domingo. He must have been a pretty good teacher, considering how well his daughter has turned out—both as a player and a person.

"I remember when I was first starting to play," Nancy Lopez recalled one day. "I asked my father for some advice. He thought for a few seconds, then he said, 'Nancy, just don't miss the ball,' and walked off to go play his shot. Come to think of it, he never really did give me many complicated things to think about."

Like most competitive kids, Nancy Lopez had a bit of a temper and wasn't always shy about displaying it on the course.

"One day I hit an awful shot and I slammed the club onto the ground," she remembers. "My father came over, looked me squarely in the eye, and said that if I ever did that again, he'd hit me with the club and that would be the end of my golf. I knew he'd never hit me, but I didn't doubt for a second that it would be the end of my golf for a long, long time."

Nancy Lopez's mother was an enthusiastic, if not necessarily good, golfer. But her contributions to her daughter's golf game were invaluable.

"We didn't have a lot of money when I was growing up," she remembers. "Dad would give my mother a little money each week for herself, and she'd save as much as she could, and then, when I was leaving to play in a tournament, she'd buy me a little golf outfit. Mom didn't understand that much about golf, but she understood love and little girls."

# LUCKY BREAKS

Ray Mangrum was playing in the 1938 PGA Championship at Shawnee Country Club, and things looked grim in his match. He was 2-down as he stood on the 17th tee and figured to be hitting the road soon.

Actually, he did, and sooner than he thought.

With out-of-bounds stakes lining the right side of the hole, Mangrum looked on in horror as he hit a huge slice off the tee. But as luck would have it, his ball landed on a concrete service road and bounded to the hole, finally coming to rest some 150 yards from the green.

Mangrum could scarcely believe his luck and took advantage of the break by hitting an 8-iron stiff to the pin. He won the 17th and 18th, then went on to win on the first extra hole.

It is one of golf's most fundamental truisms: every shot—good or bad—makes someone happy. It follows, therefore, that one guy's lucky break is someone else's bad luck. Take the case of Johnny Bulla in the 1939 British Open at St. Andrews.

Bulla finished the championship with the lead. The only man who could beat him was Richard Burton, whose approach to the home hole left him with a fifty-footer. At best, Bulla figured, Burton might two-putt for a tie. It never, ever, occurred to Bulla that Burton might sink the putt.

For that matter, it apparently never occurred to Burton, either.

"As soon as he hit the putt, he turned and began walking toward the clubhouse," said Bulla. "He never saw it go in the cup. He never even saw it get halfway to the hole."

Still, his disappointment in not winning was tempered by something that happened back in the States.

The birth of a son.

A quick look at the history of the Walker Cup Matches will tell you that, for most of its history, the team from Great Britain/Ireland could use all the lucky breaks they could get. In the 1973 matches at The Country Club in Brookline, Massachusetts, they got a great, if unlikely, break.

In a first day's alternate-shot match, John Davis hit his approach shot to the 10th green into a stand of trees. His partner, Howard Clark, tried to thread his shot back into play, but it hit a tree and bounced deeper into the woods.

In desperation, Davis hit the team's third shot through the trees and then the fun started. The ball took a big bounce off a road, then ran onto the green and into the cup for a par 4.

Alas, luck will take you only so far. In the end, the Americans won, 14–10.

One day a man named Coburn Haskell was visiting a friend who worked at the B. F. Goodrich rubber plant in Akron, Ohio.

Now, as it turned out, Haskell was a struggling golfer, and he was particularly frustrated by his lack of distance off the tee.

As luck would have it, while talking with his friend, he noticed a waste bin filled with elastic thread, and it reminded him of the threads that made up the core of a baseball.

Eureka!

Haskell wondered what would happen if you wound the rubber thread around the core of a golf ball. He went to work, trying to find out, winding hundreds of feet of elastic thread tightly around a core.

It should be noted here that Mr. Haskell must have also been a very patient man, because time after time the ball would fall from his hands and bounce wildly around the room, unraveling as it went.

But Haskell persevered, and soon he developed a ball that would go thirty yards farther than the gutta-percha balls currently in use.

The "Bouncing Billy," as it became known, changed the course of golf. It also changed Mr. Coburn Haskell's life.

He lived very comfortably ever after.

On a fall day in 1995, former New York Jets lineman Randy Rasmussen was playing golf at the Shorehaven Golf Club in Norwalk, Connecticut.

When he returned home he realized, to his horror, that he'd lost the Super Bowl ring he received as a member of the team that upset the Baltimore Colts so dramatically in 1969.

"I felt awful," said Rasmussen. "I was hoping I'd left the ring at home, but when I realized I didn't, I felt sick. I play at Shorehaven a few times every year, and every time I played, I'd try to retrace my steps, hoping I might get lucky and find my ring."

As the years went by, Rasmussen eventually gave up hope and bought a replacement ring. Still, it wasn't quite the same.

Enter Ira Miner, a Shorehaven member. Nearly five years to the day after Rasmussen lost the ring, Miner was leaving the clubhouse and spotted something in the grass, just outside the locker room. He picked it up, cleaned the dirt off, and knew he had something very special on—or in, to be more precise—his hands.

As he closely studied the ring, he recognized Rasmussen's name, which had been engraved into the ring. He called the local paper, the *Advocate*, which put him in touch with the former Jet.

"When I called him and told him I had his ring, he lost his breath," said Miner.

Later, when someone told Miner the ring could have been worth as much as $40,000, he was unfazed.

"It never occurred to me to sell the ring," said Miner. "I never even thought about it. The ring has no meaning to me. Randy is the one who worked so hard. He's the one who took a beating on the field and earned the ring. Getting the ring back to him was just the right thing to do."

# *ROGER MALTBIE*

Roger Maltbie is best known today as a member of NBC's golf team, where his insights are generously colored by his sense of humor. But he is also a fine player, who won five PGA Tour events despite twice undergoing shoulder surgery.

One of the high points of his career came in 1987, when he led the Masters going into the final round.

"I was as nervous going into that final round as I've ever been," Maltbie remembers. "Finally, my wife suggested I call my father. I did, and he told me, 'Son, it doesn't really matter what you do out there today. Your mom and I will still be very proud of you, win or lose.'

"I hung up the phone and cried for about twenty minutes," Maltbie continued. "It just purged the nervousness."

# *DAVE MARR*

Dave Marr, the 1965 PGA Champion and longtime golf analyst for both ABC and NBC Sports, was one of the most popular people in golf—in no small part because of his wit and sense of humor. He died from cancer in 1997, but even toward the end of his life, he never lost his ability to make others laugh.

One day he woke to find his wife, Tally, sitting by his bedside, softly crying.

"Mother of mercy, is this the end of Rico?" he said, mimicking Edward G. Robinson's closing line from the classic film *Little Caesar*.

"We were playing in Greensboro in 1968 when Martin Luther King was assassinated," Dave Marr once recalled. "There was a lot of debate about whether or not we should cancel the tournament. There had been some threats made, and we decided to hold a small meeting to discuss it. I wanted to cancel play because I remembered all the controversy about the NFL playing their games on the weekend after President Kennedy was killed. Arnold [Palmer] was adamant about playing. He just didn't think we should give in to threats and felt we owed it to the fans and sponsors. We went back and forth, and Arnold was in his full Arnold mode. Once he decided he wanted to do something, he could be stubborn, as they say.

"Finally, it was pretty clear Arnold was going to have his way, so I said, 'Okay, John Wayne, but let me ask you one more thing: if the shooting starts, just who do you think is going to get shot at?'

"He thought about that for a minute and agreed that maybe playing wasn't such a good idea."

Dave Marr was one of the best television golf analysts who ever lived—a fact lost on some of the geniuses who produce television sports, or write about them, who thought he wasn't critical or outspoken enough.

As though what golf needed was a second coming of Howard Cosell.

For them, it wasn't enough that Dave Marr was insightful, funny, and passionate about the game.

One year his longtime partner on the 18th tower, Jim McKay, asked him why a certain player seemed to be struggling under the pressure of the back nine on Sunday.

"Three little words, Jim," Dave Marr said. "United States Open."

In one of the great scenes from *Casablanca*, Claude Raines's character, Captain Louis Raynoud, turns to Humphrey Bogart's Rick—the cynical, hard-boiled American expatriate—and accuses him of being "nothing but a rank sentimentalist."

Like most players of his generation, Dave Marr did have a tough side. But as the wonderful writer Tom Callahan once wrote in describing Ben Crenshaw, Marr was a man who would "cry at a supermarket opening."

One such "supermarket opening" came at Baltusrol at the end of the 1980 U.S. Open.

"Jack had been in a slump and a lot of people had counted him out," Marr remembered. "When he won, a kid put 'Jack Is Back' up on the scoreboard by 18 and the gallery began chanting, 'Jack is back, Jack is back.' I started thinking about how people treated Jack when he first came out and started beating Arnold. He and Barbara had it pretty tough there for a while, and to see the warmth people showed at Baltusrol, well, it was really something. After we went off the air, I was walking back across 18 with tears in my eyes."

When the cerebrally challenged executives running ABC Sports decided to let Dave Marr go in 1991, they overlooked one small thing: he still had a year left on his contract and still had the formidable International Management Group as his agents.

Let's put it this way: when Dave Marr bid a fond farewell to ABC Sports, he took a year's worth of ABC's cash with him.

"Let's just say that if it had been a bullfight, they wouldn't have gotten an ear," Marr joked years later, when he was happily employed by NBC Sports. "It was a kill, but it wasn't a clean kill."

A writer once asked Dave Marr if he was bitter about the way he was treated by ABC Sports.

"No, I'm not," he said, breaking into a wide grin. "My evil twin, David, might be, but I'm not."

# GEORGE S. MAY

George S. May was a Chicago-area businessman who began hosting professional tournaments in 1941 as a way of promoting his Tam O'Shanter Country Club north of the city.

May had a genius for promotion. He offered record purses. He invited players from around the world. His was one of the first tournaments to provide grandstands and a scoreboard. Most important, though, he was a leader in integrating tournament golf.

"I had breakfast with George May, and he asked what he could do to improve his tournament," remembered Johnny Bulla, who played on the Tour from the 1930s into the 1960s. "There had been some black players who tried to qualify at a local private club and they weren't allowed on the course. I told him that he should invite them straight into the field. This was in the '40s, and he knew there would be people who wouldn't like having blacks in the field, but he didn't care. He knew it was the right thing to do. One man—his name was Sears, I believe—was back from serving in Europe. He hadn't been playing much, but he had tremendous talent. I believe he finished seventh, then he shipped out for the Pacific, where he was killed."

# YOUNG TOM MORRIS

When Young Tom Morris won the 1870 British Open at Prestwick, it marked his third straight Open victory, and according to the rule laid down by the Prestwick Club in 1860, he was entitled to purchase the Champion's red leather belt.

It is a testimonial to Young Tom's popularity among his fellow pros that following the championship, they passed the hat and raised the twenty-five pounds for the price of the belt—a fairly staggering sum for golf professionals in those days—and then presented it to Young Tom.

Incidentally, Young Tom's total of 149 for three rounds at the Prestwick course was never equaled in the gutta-percha-ball era.

The British Open was not played in 1871, but in 1872 Young Tom won the championship again, becoming the first player to receive the Old Claret Jug, which remains the Open trophy today. He remains the only player to win four consecutive British Open championships.

Tragically, Young Tom died on Christmas morning, 1875. He was twenty-four years old.

# MOTHER ENGLAND

At the height of the Battle of Britain, one of the fears was that the Germans would launch Hitler's long-planned invasion of the island. Should that happen, one of the first waves figured to be troops flown in by gliders.

In that case, golf courses would be likely landing sites, so the government ordered that certain precautions be taken. At the Aintree Golf Club, old cars filled with rocks were laid out across the course.

Happily, the Germans never came, but at Aintree at least, the golfers certainly did. When the war ended, the cars were removed and workers started to restore the course. When they did, they found hundreds of golf balls. It seems it took more than a little thing like World War II to keep the British away from their beloved game.

Percy Belgrave "Laddie" Lucas was a British Walker Cup player and captain who distinguished himself as an often-decorated fighter pilot in the Royal Air Force during World War II.

On one mission, his plane was badly shot up in a battle over the English Channel. When he made it back over land, he began to look for a place to land his crippled Spitfire. Happily, he spotted a familiar site—Prince's—the course where Gene Sarazen won the 1932 British Open. He set the plane down on the first fairway but soon ran out of land and ended up in a swamp.

"I never could hit that fairway," said Lucas, who did the only logical—and typically British—thing after climbing out of the wreckage. He walked up to the clubhouse, introduced himself, apologized for any inconvenience he may have caused, and ordered a large gin.

The 1959 Great Britain/Ireland Ryder Cup team was almost killed when their flight from Los Angeles to Palm Springs was caught in a massive electrical storm and went into a violent and frightening free fall over the mountains. So terrifying was the incident that the players insisted the plane return to Los Angeles, where they boarded a bus and were driven to Palm Springs.

The Americans prevailed in the Ryder Cup, 8½–3½, but even in defeat, the Great Britain/Ireland boys showed their class. After the matches, each member of the team received an elegant card inscribed with the following:

"Being a founding member of the club [of which only team members belonged], you have a high position to uphold. To avoid the risk of dropping low in the eyes of the other cofounders, you must raise your glass and toast each and every one of them at 5:30 P.M. on 20 October every year you are lucky to remain alive, which you are lucky to be at the moment."

October 20 is the anniversary of the team's brush with death.

Argentina's Vicente Fernandez was a popular player on the European circuit, but when the Falklands War between England and Argentina broke out in 1982, the Argentinean government refused to let Fernandez travel to Europe for several months.

Once the war ended, Fernandez traveled to the Benson and Hedges Championship at York, where he had won in 1975. There was some concern about how the British fans might treat Fernandez.

There shouldn't have been any.

"I was playing the last hole in the first round, and as I approached the green, there must have been thirty thousand people in the grandstands shouting my name and calling, 'Welcome back, Vicente.' I was so emotional, every part of my body was shaking. I don't know how I finished the hole. Even today, I do not have any of my trophies in my home, but I do have some British newspaper stories of my welcome back framed and hung on the wall. I will always remember how kind the British people were to me that day."

# THE NATIONAL GOLF LINKS

Charles Blair Macdonald was understandably proud of his work in designing the National Golf Links on Long Island. Perhaps just a tad too proud.

Now, Macdonald was certainly no shrinking violet when it came to the ego department, but he may have outdone himself when he commissioned a life-size, bronze statue of himself for the club—and then billed it to the membership.

# *BYRON NELSON*

By every account, Byron Nelson is one of the most respected and beloved players golf has ever produced. As Ken Venturi has often said, you can argue all day who the greatest golfer of all time is, but there's no question that Byron is the greatest gentleman who ever rose to the top of the game. That's what makes this story a cautionary tale for all those who elect to swim in the murky and perilous waters of television.

"Byron had been the lead analyst for ABC for a long time, and by the late 1970s he wanted to cut back a little bit so he could spend more time with his [late] wife Louise at the ranch," remembered Dave Marr, who was at ABC Sports at the time and was hardly naive about the world in which he worked. "He wrote to Roone [Arledge, the head of ABC Sports] and asked if he could reduce the number of tournaments he was required to work. He never heard back, so as the first tournament of the year approached, he called New York and asked one of the production assistants about the travel arrangements. The kid kind of gulped and said he'd get back to him. Finally, one of Roone's assistants called and told Byron he was being let go. I thought, Is this how you treat a man like Byron Nelson? You just stop sending the limo? It just broke his heart. I figured, if they can do that to a Byron Nelson, what can they do to a Dave Marr?"

Incidentally, as it turned out, Marr found out a little over a decade later when, in 1991, he learned from a friend that ABC was planning to replace him with Steve Melnyk.

After the final round of that fall's Tour Championship at Pinehurst, an ABC executive, Dennis Lewin, asked Marr to come to his hotel room.

He didn't tell Marr the reason for the visit.

He didn't need to.

"That was one long walk," Marr said. "I felt like Jimmy Cagney on the way to the electric chair in one of those old gangster movies."

# JACK NICKLAUS

Even as a kid, Jack Nicklaus had a remarkable work ethic. "When Jack was fifteen, he played in his first Ohio Open," his teacher, the late Jack Grout, once recalled. "He shot a 63, which was a course record, and won the tournament, beating a lot of good players. The next day he came to my shop, and I asked him to tell me about his round. He gave me the hole-by-hole. I congratulated him and asked him what he was going to do for the rest of the day. I figured that, like most kids, he would take the day off and enjoy his win. He gave me a funny look and said, 'Geez, Mr. Grout. I'm gonna practice.'"

Jack Nicklaus took his first golf lesson in the summer of 1951 and shot a 51 for his first nine holes of golf. A few months later he shot a 91, and a short while after that, he won his first tournament—the Scioto Country Club Junior Championship.

"I threw a 121 at the field and they folded," Nicklaus recalled later, laughing.

It's been said that Jack Nicklaus is even more gracious in defeat than he is in victory, and that is most certainly true. It's also true that even in times of his greatest disappointments, he's unfailingly professional in his dealings with the press.

In 1962, he came to The Country Club outside Boston to defend his U.S. Open title. Although few knew it at the time (Nicklaus is also known for never making excuses), he was suffering from a sore, stiff neck, and it showed in his play. For one of the few times in the prime of his career, he missed the cut in the Open.

Still, writers have to write about something, so they requested that Nicklaus come for an interview for the second day in a row.

"You guys must be crazy," Nicklaus said, "talking to a 76 yesterday and a 77 today."

For all his considerable strengths, Jack Nicklaus's greatest competitive weapon might be his mind. His ability to concentrate and block out all distractions is unequaled. Witness his decision to quit smoking on the golf course.

One day, while watching a highlight film of his victory over Arnold Palmer in the 1962 U.S. Open, Nicklaus decided he didn't like the example he was setting—especially among youngsters—by smoking. So, Nicklaus being Nicklaus, he simply stopped smoking on the course, while still smoking a pack a day.

"I asked Jack how he could smoke twenty cigarettes a day but not smoke in the heat of competition," recalls his longtime friend and collaborator Ken Bowden. "He just looked at me and said, 'Kenny, I never think about it.'"

Contrast that with the fits Arnold Palmer suffered in his decade-long struggle to quit. In typical Palmer fashion, his millions of fans followed his battle with butts like soap opera fans agonizing over the travails of their favorite characters.

# CHRISTY O'CONNOR, SR.

Himself, as Christy O'Connor was affectionately known, was one of the best golfers Europe produced in the post–World War II era. He was an enormous talent, posting a second in the 1965 British Open, along with several other high finishes. Happily, his love for the game was matched only by his love for life and whatever good times came along the way.

In the 1973 Ryder Cup Matches at Muirfield, O'Connor lost to J. C. Snead in the morning matches of the final day. Disappointed, he told the Great Britain/Ireland captain, Bernard Hunt, that he wanted to be left out of the afternoon matches, preferring to follow the course of play from the comfort of the bar.

Upon reflection, Hunt decided that he wanted Himself to take on the formidable Tom Weiskopf in the afternoon and implored O'Connor's wife, Mary, to get the old boy out of his chair and onto the first tee in plenty of time.

"Ordinarily, a player with a few drinks under his belt wouldn't be of much use," said Hunt. "But Christy was capable of the most remarkable golf under these conditions. The problem was that if the effects of the drink began to wear off, Christy could lose his edge."

To guard against this calamity, Hunt pulled aside two of O'Connor's friends—one of whom happened to be a priest and, therefore, had the further attraction of bringing God into the fray—and gave them a job of immeasurable importance.

"Whatever you do," he told them, with more than a hint of conspiracy in his voice, "keep Himself topped off."

To that end, they agreed to meet Christy on every tee with a little liquid something, just in case of an emergency.

When O'Connor arrived on the first tee, he shook hands with Weiskopf, who thought there was something strange going on.

"I kind of took Bernard aside and asked him if Christy had been drinking," Weiskopf recalled. "He looked at me, smiled, and said, 'God yes, and if we can keep him that way you don't stand a chance.'"

As it turned out, Himself, suitably fortified, played Weiskopf to a tie, but in the end the United States prevailed, 19–13.

# JOSE MARIA OLAZABAL

Jose Maria Olazabal's victory in the 1999 Masters Tournament marked the culmination of his comeback from a mysterious ailment that left him unable to walk, let alone play golf.

As an amateur, he had won the British Boys', Junior, and Amateur Championships. Between 1990 and 1994, he won the Masters, two NEC World Series of Golf tournaments, and the International, all on the PGA Tour. He won numerous international events and was a mainstay on five European Ryder Cup teams.

In 1995, he had surgery to remove part of a bone from one of his feet. An examination at the Mayo Clinic misdiagnosed him with rheumatoid arthritis, and his future was very much in doubt.

But in 1997, a German doctor ordered a combination of diet and exercise changes, and within three months Olazabal could walk without pain. Six months after the exam, he was playing competitively on the European Tour.

Late in 1997, he was a key member of the European Ryder Cup team that beat the Americans at Valderrama, in his native Spain.

At the postmatch press conference, all the members of the victorious team talked about their feelings. When it was Olazabal's turn, he stood and clenched the table with both hands until his knuckles whitened.

"This is very special for me," he said as tears welled in his eyes. "One year ago, I could not even walk. And now, for this . . ."

With that he sat down and sobbed, as teammates came to his side and comforted their friend.

In 1985, Olazabal won the silver medal as the low amateur at the British Open at Royal St. Georges. He finished seven strokes behind the champion, Sandy Lyle, and beat the likes of Ben Crenshaw, Tom Watson, Nick Faldo, and fellow Spaniard Seve Ballesteros.

After the championship, he was asked how it felt to be the "next Ballesteros."

"I don't want to be the next Ballesteros," he said. "I want to be the first Olazabal."

# *FRANCIS OUIMET*

Golf has been blessed in that so many of the game's great champions have also been great sportsmen (and sportswomen). Certainly, Francis Ouimet, who won the 1913 U.S. Open as an amateur, would fall into that category.

Ouimet, who also won two U.S. Amateurs, played on eight Walker Cup teams, and served as team captain twice, was the first American honored as captain of the Royal & Ancient Golf Club of St. Andrews.

No less a figure than Bob Jones summed up Ouimet, the player and the man, when he wrote:

"As one who was first his awed admirer, later his fellow competitor, and now, as always, his staunch friend, I salute him with all possible fervor."

Francis Ouimet must have had a very patient and loving mother, bless her heart.

Young Francis first became attracted to golf in grade school, when he used to take a shortcut from home to school

111

across The Country Club. It wasn't long before he started caddying and became hooked on the game.

As luck would have it, Ouimet's shortcut also provided him with a golden opportunity to search for golf balls. One late-fall day, Ouimet returned home with a pocket filled with balls and decided to see what would happen if he heated them in the oven.

Sad to report, he forgot about the balls and went out to play with some friends from the neighborhood. When his poor, sainted mother returned home, the house was filled with smoke from the balls, which had been reduced to a gooey mess.

For some mothers, that would have marked the end of her son's infatuation with the game, but not for Mrs. Ouimet.

She did, however, give young Francis a stern talking-to that he remembered for the rest of his life.

In 1963, the U.S. Open returned to The Country Club on the fiftieth anniversary of Ouimet's victory. On the eve of the championship, the club hosted a dinner for the presidents and professionals from Massachusetts clubs.

During the course of the evening, people were asked to guess what they thought would be the winning score. The guests, no doubt in awe of players like Arnold Palmer and Jack Nicklaus, suggested that the scores would be on the low side.

Most woefully underestimated the character and resolve of "The Old Lady of Clyde Street." One who didn't was Francis Ouimet.

"Gentlemen," Ouimet said. "I will remind you that this is a very subtle course."

Subtle indeed.

The low score at the end of four rounds was 293—nine over par and four over the highest guess of the evening. In all, par was broken just five times in regulation play and was never broken in the eighteen holes played on the final day.

Francis Ouimet and Gene Sarazen were great friends and competitors, and when Ouimet died, his family asked Sarazen to serve as a pallbearer.

"At the church the day of the funeral, I was thinking about Francis and how, just before the Open, he always said to me, 'Gene, make sure those greens are fast.' After the service, when it came time to say good-bye to Francis, I tapped on the coffin, bent down, and whispered, 'Francis, make sure those greens are fast up there.'"

# ARNOLD PALMER

Arnold Palmer's father, Deacon, was a stern, no-nonsense man who instilled in his son a deep and abiding love for the game. He also instilled a strict sense of right and wrong.

Deacon Palmer was the greenkeeper and golf professional at the Latrobe Country Club, and young Arnold spent his days around the course, working on the grounds and as a caddie.

One of the rules was that caddies were forbidden to hit balls on the course except on specific days. A rule like that is made to be broken, and sure enough, one day Arnold was caught hitting balls. The second it happened, he knew he was in trouble.

A well-meaning man suggested that an appropriate punishment might be for Arnold to go spend some time working in the nearby steel mills.

"I'll raise my son the way I want him to be raised," Deacon Palmer said firmly, marking the end of the discussion.

When Arnold Palmer was twelve years old, he broke 80 for the first time. Naturally, he was very proud of this great accomplishment and couldn't help bragging just a bit.

Bragging was not something that sat well with his father.

"When you're good, you don't have to tell people what you can do," Deacon Palmer said. "Just show them."

Like most kids, Arnold Palmer longed for his parents' approval. In the case of his golf game, he was particularly eager to please his father, whose praise was hard to come by.

Deacon Palmer's job prevented him from taking time to go watch his son play in many junior tournaments. One day, however, he did go watch Arnold play.

As luck would have it, Arnold wasn't having one of his best days. In frustration after missing another putt, he threw his putter over a tree.

Big mistake.

There was a stony silence after the round and in the car on the drive home. Finally, Deacon Palmer let his son know what he thought of his antics.

He told him if he ever saw his son throw another club, it would be the end of his fledgling golf career.

Arnold Palmer is notorious for his tinkering with clubs, to the point where he'd often rework his leather grips in between shots. Sometimes, his fascination with equipment became almost comical.

"I always felt sorry for Arnold's caddies," said Bob Rosburg. "Arnold would show up with four or five putters, a couple sets of irons, and three or four drivers. For a guy who was so decisive about everything else, he sure had a hard time making up his mind about his clubs."

Arnold Palmer's victory in the 1960 Masters was easily one of the most dramatic moments in a career marked by dramatic triumphs and losses.

Trying to catch and pass Ken Venturi, Palmer ran in a forty-footer for a birdie on 17 to get into a tie. Then, on 18, he sank a six-footer for another birdie and the victory. Later, Clifford Roberts asked him if he'd like to stay over and play with President Eisenhower. Naturally, Palmer was delighted and eagerly agreed.

When he was introduced to the President the following day, Ike warmly shook his hand.

"It's a pleasure to meet you," the president said to Palmer. "I hear you're a pretty good putter."

Arnold Palmer made his first British Open appearance at St. Andrews in 1960, finishing second by a stroke to Australia's Kel Nagle. He returned the following year at Royal

Birkdale and encountered some of the worst weather in the history of the championship.

"It was almost scary out there," said Palmer years later. "The exhibition tents were flattened and full kegs of beer were flying through the air. The R&A wanted to call the championship off. They really felt it would be too dangerous to play. But I was one of the players who argued that, weather or no weather, we should play. What was I going to do, come back home and tell everyone that I went over to win this prestigious championship and it was canceled?"

Thirty years after his first visit to both St. Andrews and the British Open, Palmer returned for his final appearance. He and his wife, Winnie, stayed in the same room they always stayed in at Rusacks Hotel, and when he opened with rounds of 71 and 73, he seemed certain to make the cut.

But in the back of his mind, Palmer was concerned. After an emotional final trip across the Swilcan Bridge on the 18th hole, Palmer left his birdie putt on 18 just inches short, and had to settle for a par.

Finally, late in the day, Palmer got the bad news. The cut had been the lowest in the championship's history, and he'd missed it by a stroke.

When he received the news, Arnold Palmer sat in his room and cried freely.

# GARY PLAYER

Gary Player never harbored many—if any—doubts about his future success, but as a young assistant professional in his native South Africa, he knew he had to leave home and try his luck in Great Britain.

So it was, then, that he scraped together his £100 in earnings (earned at a princely 30 pence per half-hour lesson) and a £100 stake from the membership and headed for the 1955 British Open at St. Andrews.

En route, he stopped in Cairo and won the Egyptian Match Play Championship—and a much-needed £300 winner's check.

When he arrived in St. Andrews, he realized that even with his winnings, a hotel room was going to be a luxury, so he spent several nights sleeping in his rainsuit out among the dunes.

"It wasn't a great hardship," Player said years later. "Many people endure such conditions every night of their life."

A nice man named Gustav Lesser wrote with a story that captures a little bit of Gary Player's spirit.

It seems that Mr. Lesser was working as a volunteer at the 1989 U.S. Open, and during a practice round he was working at the 11th tee. The threesome of Arnold Palmer, Jim Gallagher, Jr., and Gary Player arrived on the tee, followed by an enormous gallery.

After Gallagher drove, he walked over to the tee bench and sat down. A youngster politely asked for his autograph, and Gallagher happily signed.

After Palmer drove, Gallagher called over to him and asked him to sign an autograph for the boy. Palmer signed the boy's book.

After Player hit his tee shot, the boy politely called out, "Please, Mr. Player, can I have your autograph?"

With that, Player turned to the boy, stared at him, and sternly said, "Son, I only give autographs to my friends."

The boy—along with most of the gallery in earshot—were in shock.

Then, after a brief pause, he walked over to the rope, took the boy's little hand in both of his, and said, "And you are now my friend."

A fter Jose Maria Olazabal's dramatic victory in the 1999 Masters, he happily gave a share of the credit to a conversation with Gary Player at the tournament's Champions Dinner, which is held on the eve of the first round.

Olazabal's career had been sidelined by a mysterious and misdiagnosed foot ailment, which made it impossible for him to play golf. Indeed, sometimes he was in so much pain he struggled to get out of bed in the morning.

But the 1994 champion arrived at the Masters completely cured—if not exactly the most confident player in the field. That's where Player came into the picture.

When he saw Olazabal at the dinner, he asked the Spaniard how he was playing.

"Okay. So-so. Not so great," Olazabal said. "Really, not so bad."

Player asked how his confidence was.

"It's not really great," Olazabal replied.

"You know, you have a great swing," Player said. "If you didn't, I wouldn't tell you this. You must believe in yourself. Look at what I've been able to do because I believe in myself. If you play eighteen holes, but don't play well, it doesn't matter. Just go to the driving range or go putt and fix the problem. This is how you achieve greatness."

Player's comments—coupled with his belief in Olazabal—made all the difference.

"He was so passionate, he made me believe in myself again," said Olazabal.

# POLITICIANS

It's safe to say that the late, great Thomas P. "Tip" O'Neill had a cordial, but not exactly close, relationship with President Jimmy Carter.

Tip was the Speaker of the House. Jimmy Carter was a president who didn't exactly love wheeling and dealing with pols.

Tip was a Boston Irish Catholic who understood the weaknesses of the human spirit. Jimmy Carter was a Southern Baptist who tended to take a pretty stern view of the human condition.

Tip was known to take a drink now and then. Jimmy Carter? Well, no.

Tip loved golf. Jimmy Carter ran in road races and set the schedule for the White House tennis court.

And on and on and on . . .

One day Tip was playing in a pro-am to help raise money to fight heart disease. When he reached the 6th green, a cart pulled up and a young man from the pro shop staff breathlessly told the Speaker that the President wanted to speak with him.

"Is it important?" Tip asked

"I don't know, sir," the kid said. "All I know is that it's the president."

"Tell him I'll call him at the turn," said Tip, who then went on to make his putt.

True to his word, when he putted out on the 9th hole, Tip went into the pro shop and called the White House, only to be told that the President was busy.

"Well," said the Speaker. "Tell him that unless there's a war, I'll talk to him after my round."

J ack Kennedy may have been the most accomplished golfer to have ever lived in the White House. But since the Democrats had made such a big deal about President Dwight Eisenhower's passion for the game, he went to great pains to hide both his ability and love for the game.

One day, he took a break from campaigning for a round with his old friend, Red Fay. On one par 3, it looked as though Kennedy's tee shot would drop into the hole. Instead, it rolled past the hole, stopping just inches away.

"Tough break, Jack," Fay said.

"Are you kidding?" Kennedy quipped. "Do you have any idea how much it would have cost my old man to keep that quiet?"

P resident Dwight Eisenhower was a passionate golfer, and his favorite place to play was Augusta National, usually with the club's longtime chairman, Clifford Roberts.

Roberts was a close friend of the president's and was instrumental in securing the Republican nomination for Eisenhower in 1952. He was also a shrewd businessman who took an active role in Eisenhower's investments. It's safe to say that Ike trusted Cliff Roberts implicitly . . . at least, to a point.

One day Eisenhower, Roberts, and two other Augusta National members were playing the par-3 12th hole. In those days, there wasn't a pond guarding the front of the green. Instead, it was just a part of Rae's Creek.

Ike's tee shot came up short, and when the foursome reached the creek, the President's ball was resting on a small sandbar.

"I think you can play it from there," Roberts told his partner, the most powerful man on the face of the earth.

With that, Ike gingerly walked down into the creek bed and onto the sandbar.

As the Secret Service officers looked on in horror, the aforementioned most powerful man on the face of the earth began to sink. He was already over his knees when the officers raced to his side and struggled to pull him out.

After returning to the clubhouse to change his clothes, Eisenhower rejoined his friends.

"That's the last time I'll ever listen to you when it comes to golf," Ike told Roberts.

Golfers playing the 10th hole at the Myopia Hunt Club outside Boston can thank—or curse—former president

William Howard Taft if their ball finds the treacherous bunker that bears Taft's name.

According to legend, Taft was a friend of Herbert Leeds, who designed Myopia. Whenever Taft managed to play safely from the bunker, Leeds would order workmen to dig it even deeper.

Eventually, the crew got it deep enough to please Leeds and torment generations of players who followed.

# THE PRESS

Bernard Darwin remains one of the game's most respected writers, but he was also talented enough as a player to compete in the 1932 Walker Cup at The Country Club outside Boston.

For all his skill, however, he was under no delusions about how far you could go with talent alone. In one match, when he faced a particularly difficult shot, he turned his eyes to the heavens and said, "Lord, this is no job for the boy. You better come yourself."

Dan Jenkins has covered professional golf since the 1950s, first for the Fort Worth *Star-Telegram*, then for *Sports Illustrated*, and now for *Golf Digest*. His novel about the Tour, *Dead Solid Perfect*, is a classic.

By any standard, Dan Jenkins is widely admired and even copied by other writers, but his place in the game was solidified at the 1999 Ryder Cup, when former president George Bush stopped by the pressroom to visit Jenkins.

"That makes Dan the greatest writer ever," one of his fellow writers quipped. "Do you think the king ever came by to visit Bernard Darwin?"

While President Bush was visiting the pressroom, his wife, Barbara, was being introduced to one of the true characters in the world of golf, "Tiny" Harike.

Tiny, who as you might expect is anything but, is a large, powerful man seldom seen without a cigar clenched firmly between his teeth. He has worked for decades at the Masters, where he keeps the riffraff out of the pressroom. He is so imposing and, therefore so good at his job, that he frequently works at other events.

And so it was that he was seated outside the pressroom at The Country Club when Mrs. Bush approached, looking for her husband. As she started through the door, Tiny stopped her and asked for her credential.

The patrician Mrs. Bush was momentarily taken aback, until her Secret Service detail rushed to her rescue.

But giving credit where credit is due, Mrs. Bush should have been flattered: Tiny knew from just one look that she was no sportswriter.

If it wasn't for a timely phone call from an editor at *Sports Illustrated*, Judy Rankin might never have become one of the game's finest champions and most intelligent television golf analysts.

As an eight-year-old, she pored over newspaper accounts of Ben Hogan's victory in the 1953 British Open at Carnoustie. Six years later, she made headlines of her own by becoming the youngest winner of the Missouri Amateur, and a year later, she was the low amateur in the U.S. Women's Open.

This was all heady stuff, and when, in 1961, the sixteen-year-old Judy Torluemke headed for the Ladies' British Open Amateur Championship (the very proper British name for the championship) at Carnoustie, it was with the highest of expectations.

Alas, her hopes were dashed when she was beaten, 1-up, in just the second round. She returned home to St. Louis and vowed never to play golf again.

Happily, a few weeks later the fateful call came from New York. The editor asked if she was entered in the U.S. Women's Open. If so, he said, *Sports Illustrated* was planning to put her on the cover, based on her finish a year before.

It took young Judy about a nanosecond to come out of retirement. She graced the cover, turned pro a year later, and went on to win twenty-six LPGA tournaments before chronic back problems forced her off the Tour in the early 1980s.

Still, if it hadn't been for that call . . .

In 1937, the American Ryder Cup team traveled to South-port & Ainsdale Golf Club in Southport, England. Among the team members was a young Byron Nelson, who was playing in his first Ryder Cup Matches.

When the American captain, Walter Hagen, announced his pairings, the British press had a field day.

"Hagen paired me and Ed Dudley against Henry Cotton and Alf Padgham, who was the British Open champion at the time," Nelson remembered. "The day of our match, the headline in one of the papers read, 'Hagen Feeds Lambs to the Butcher.' Well, we won the match pretty easily, and the next day the headline was 'The Lambs Bit the Butcher.' I got quite a kick out of that."

# NICK PRICE

Nick Price, the winner of two PGA Championships and a British Open, is universally regarded as one of the nicest guys in golf. He's unfailingly pleasant and accommodating, which, given the demands on his time, makes him all the more remarkable.

In 1990, he hired Jeff "Squeeky" Medlin as his caddie, and the two enjoyed considerable success and developed a deep and abiding affection for each other.

At the 1994 British Open at Turnberry, Price came to the final hole needing a par to beat Jesper Parnevik by a stroke. After hitting a good drive, Price safely hit the green and began the traditional champion's walk to the green, with the gallery spilling onto the fairway, engulfing the players and their caddies.

When Price and Squeeky broke through the gallery, Price noticed that Squeeky was lingering behind.

"Come on, Squeek," he said. "Let's enjoy this together. We might never have the chance again."

And so the two friends walked together to the green, the roar of the enormous gallery echoing in their ears.

Sadly, Price's words proved all too prescient.

Squeeky died in 1997 after a courageous battle with leukemia.

# TED RAY

Ted Ray, who won the 1912 British Open and the 1920 U.S. Open, is most familiar to American golfers as the man who, along with Harry Vardon, lost to Francis Ouimet in a playoff for the 1913 U.S. Open at The Country Club in Brookline, Massachusetts.

On the day of the playoff, ten thousand locals flocked to the course (in no small part because the Open didn't charge admission fees in those days) to cheer on the twenty-year-old Ouimet—a Townie, as we say in Boston—who grew up across Clyde Street from the 17th green. Now, it's safe to say that even the impeccably behaved Boston sports fans of the day knew little about golf or about how they should behave on the course, so there were bound to be a few disruptions.

At one point a rules official loudly admonished a man in the gallery—just as Ray prepared to hit his putt.

"Sir, are you going to talk or am I going to putt?" Ray asked sternly.

# CHI CHI RODRIGUEZ

Chi Chi Rodriguez is passionate in his devotion to kids, especially underprivileged kids. He's especially interested in exposing them to golf, in no small part because it was his path out of wrenching poverty as a child growing up in Puerto Rico.

One day he was talking to a child who had demonstrated some skill for the game.

"What do you want to be when you grow up?" Chi Chi asked the child.

"I want to be a pro," the child said.

"Why?" Chi Chi asked.

"Because I want to win tournaments and become very rich and famous," he said. "I want everything."

"The problem with wanting everything, son," Chi Chi said, "is that it's never enough."

Vicente Fernandez is best known for his fine play on the Senior Tour, but in the early '60s, he was a struggling young player in his native Argentina. His father had been severely injured in an accident, and the family struggled to get by. While Vicente was a player of obvious talent and desire, golf was a dicey proposition for a family that needed money.

To make matters worse, the Argentinean PGA ruled that members had to be at least eighteen, and non-PGA members were banned from all but "Open" tournaments. Increasingly, Fernandez was being pressured by his family to give up this golf foolishness and go to work as an apprentice tailor.

As luck would have it, the World Cup came to Argentina in 1962, and as the National Caddy Champion, Fernandez was assigned as Chi Chi Rodriguez's caddie.

In the course of the tournament, Rodriguez became impressed with the young man and was tremendously moved by the story of his struggles to compete and provide for his family. He was so moved, in fact, that he offered to adopt Fernandez and have him move to Puerto Rico, where Rodriguez would arrange for a job and playing opportunities.

A grateful Fernandez took Rodriguez up on his offer, and his parents reluctantly agreed. By early 1963, the adoption papers were in order and Fernandez was ready to move. Within days, however, the Argentinean PGA changed their bylaws and Fernandez was allowed to join. Later that year, he finished second in his country's PGA Championship, losing to the great Roberto de Vicenzo.

His success was far from assured, and he would struggle for many more years, but the finish proved—to him and to others—that he truly could compete with the best players in the world.

# BOB ROSBURG

There are television golf analysts who get more airtime and more publicity than Bob Rosburg, but there's no one better at sizing up a situation succinctly than the 1959 PGA champion.

As a player, Rossie was known for moving right along, not wasting time. The same was pretty much true in 1984, when ABC golf producer Terry Jastrow asked him to take newcomer Judy Rankin out on the course to show her the intricacies of being an on-course reporter.

"He took me out and said, 'This is where you stand on a par 4,'" Rankin remembers. "Then we moved to another hole, and he said, 'This is where you stand on a par 5.' I asked him about the par 3s, and he said I could stand wherever I wanted. They were short holes."

With that, Rossie proved what many people suspected all along: being an on-course reporter may pay well, but it's not brain surgery.

# THE ROYAL & ANCIENT GOLF CLUB OF ST. ANDREWS

Tom Kite was a member of the 1971 Walker Cup team. On the flight to St. Andrews, the twenty-one-year-old Kite talked with his veteran teammate Bill Campbell about the Walker Cup in general and St. Andrews specifically.

"I asked him whether St. Andrews was hilly or flat," Kite recalls. "He said, 'Yes.'

"After I played it for the first time in a practice round, I realized just how perfect his answer was."

Apparently, St. Andrews agreed with Kite. He won both his singles matches and teamed with Campbell to get a half in the foursomes.

Old Tom Morris, the first professional at St. Andrews, was a wonderful player who won four British Opens in the early years of the championship. But like almost all golfers, he occasionally had problems with his putting.

One time a friend sent him a letter. It was addressed simply:

> To the Misser of Short Putts
> St. Andrews, Scotland

# THE RULES

John Adams was playing in the Pan American Open in Costa Rica and approached Glen Tait, a longtime PGA Tour rules official, with a question.

"Glen, what's the rule on receiving advice?" Adams asked.

"What's the situation?" Tait asked.

"Well, I've been talking to this rock for the last five holes and I've made three birdies," Adams said.

"Well, if you birdie the next four holes, loan it to me," Tait said. "I want to talk to it, too."

In the 1947 Ryder Cup Matches, in Portland, Oregon, the captain of the Great Britain/Ireland team, Henry Cotton, suspected that the American team was using clubs with scoring grooves that were deeper than the rules allowed. After an inspection, officials ruled that the grooves—and the clubs—were just fine.

Fast-forward two years, to the matches at Ganton in Yorkshire, England. The American captain, Ben Hogan—who played in the 1947 matches—requested that officials check to see if the grooves on the irons of Dai Rees and Dick Burton were illegal.

This time, it turned out they were, although the exercise didn't do much for Anglo-American golf relations.

In the 1956 PGA Championship at the Blue Hills Golf and Country Club near Boston, Doug Ford, the defending champion, was in a tough match against Mike Deitz in the second round.

Ford was 1-up playing the 15th hole but hit his drive into the woods. He played a fine pitch out of the trees and watched as the ball rolled onto the green.

Standing in the fairway, Dietz couldn't see the green, so he called to spectators, asking how far Ford's ball was from the hole.

Ford immediately charged Dietz with a violation of Rule 9, which states that "a player shall not give or ask for advice, or take any action which may result in his receiving advice except from his caddie, his partner, or his partner's caddie."

Shaken, Dietz went on to make a four to win the hole, but the referee agreed with Ford and awarded the hole to the defending champion.

Now 2-up with three holes to play, Ford lost the 16th and 18th, and the match went to sudden death. He finally won on the fifth playoff hole when he holed a wedge from forty yards out but lost in the afternoon to another former PGA Champion, Walter Burkemo, 5 & 3.

All of which only proves that while the rules can be your friend, knowing them doesn't always help you keep the friends you have.

A similar ruling cost the Great Britain/Ireland team in the 1971 Ryder Cup at Old Warson Country Club in St. Louis.

Playing the par-3 7th hole in the second day's foursomes match, Arnold Palmer laced his tee shot close to the pin.

"Great shot," said Bernard Gallacher's caddie. "What did you hit?"

"Five-iron," said Palmer.

All this would have been fine, and innocent enough, if the match's referee hadn't overheard the caddie. After the hole was halved with pars, the referee awarded the hole to Palmer and his partner, Gardner Dickinson, which put them 2-up.

Not that it mattered all that much. In the end, Palmer and Dickinson breezed to an easy 5 & 4 victory.

# THE RYDER CUP

In 1967, Ben Hogan, the captain of the American team, caused a stir at the pretournament dinner when he introduced his charges by simply saying: "Ladies and gentlemen, I'd like to introduce the twelve best players in the world, the United States Ryder Cup team."

With that, Hogan sat down and the Americans went on to prove that, if not exactly tactful, Hogan was nevertheless right on the mark. His team won, 23½–8½.

Twenty-two years later, at the Belfry in Sutton Coldfield, England, the American captain, Raymond Floyd, stood up at the pretournament dinner and repeated Hogan's introduction. This took considerably more nerve than it did when Hogan said it, given the fact that the Americans had lost the previous two matches.

Miffed, European captain Tony Jacklin turned to a friend and said, "What am I supposed to say, 'I'd like to introduce the thirteenth-best player in the world, Seve Ballesteros?'"

Even a cursory look at the history of the Ryder Cup shows that, until recent years, the Americans dominated the event. To a large degree, this was due to superior American skill and depth, but occasionally the Yanks could use the stubbornness—even stupidity—of British PGA officials for their good fortune.

A case in point was the 1931 matches at Scioto Country Club in Columbus, Ohio, when the Americans breezed to a 9–3 victory. There's no doubt the matches would have been closer if three of the Great Britain/Ireland players hadn't been excluded from the team.

At that time, the rules stated that team members must be both natives and residents of the country they represented. That disqualified Percy Alliss, who had a lucrative club job at Berlin's Wansee Club, and Aubrey Boomer, who was at St. Cloud outside Paris.

Then there was the matter of the sometimes-imperious Cotton, who told officials he wished to stay in the States following the matches and play in tournaments and exhibitions. The British PGA refused. Cotton offered to pay his own way, but again, the officials said no.

With that, Cotton threatened to quit the team. The PGA offered a compromise, letting Cotton stay in the States but only as a member of the PGA contingent.

Too little, too late. By that time, Cotton had agreed to join Alliss and Boomer in a series of lucrative exhibitions in the States.

They made a lot of money.

Their teammates got clobbered.

Today, the Ryder Cup is one of the biggest events in all of sports, let alone golf. But that wasn't always the case. Take the 1959 matches in Palm Springs.

When the team from Great Britain and Ireland arrived at the Eldorado Country Club for their practice rounds, they discovered that not only was the course still open for member play, but the members who were playing had no intention of letting them play through.

One of the closest and most dramatic Ryder Cup Matches in history occurred in 1933 at Southport and Ainsdale Golf Club in Southport, England. The matches literally came down to the last putt of the last match.

America's Denny Shute and England's Syd Easterbrook came to the 18th hole tied in their singles match. Shute, who faced a putt of some four feet, was slightly away and made his putt. That left it all up to Easterbrook, who was only inches inside Shute.

The enormous gallery had settled around the green, and after a roar when Shute's ball fell into the cup, it became eerily silent. Easterbrook carefully studied his putt, which broke sharply from left to right.

Then he made it.

"I remember thinking, 'Better him than me,'" said Shute years later. "But he holed it like a man and the cup was theirs, fair and square."

The 1957 Ryder Cup Matches at the Lindrick Golf Club at Lindrick, Yorkshire, was the scene of one of the ugliest confrontations in the Cup's long history.

American Dow Finsterwald, who would win the PGA Championship the following year, faced Ireland's Christy O'Connor, Sr., in a singles match.

On the third hole, Finsterwald—who was already 2-down—missed a six-footer for a win, then walked to the hole and picked up his ball, which was clearly within tap-in range.

"Mr. O'Connor, 3-up!" said the referee, awarding the hole to the Irishman because Finsterwald picked up his ball without the putt having been conceded.

Finsterwald was incensed, and the atmosphere was chilly to the point of frigid.

It reached the frigid point on the 9th hole of the afternoon round, when O'Connor missed a short putt for a win, then picked up his ball and headed for the 10th tee.

As O'Connor prepared to tee off, Finsterwald called out, "Hold it." Then he argued that since O'Connor had picked up his ball without the putt having been conceded, Finsterwald had won the hole.

At this point in the match, however, it scarcely mattered.

O'Connor closed out Finsterwald, 7 & 6.

The two men left the course without shaking hands, and no amount of pleading from their teammates could restore the men's sense of sportsmanship.

It wasn't, as they say, a moment for the Ryder Cup highlight reel.

# GENE SARAZEN

In 1982, *Golf Digest* asked Dave Anderson, the Pulitzer prize–winning *New York Times* sports columnist, to collaborate with Gene Sarazen on a listing of the ten greatest male and female golfers of the century. Since Sarazen, then age eighty, had either played with or seen every great player of that span, he was the perfect choice.

Sarazen labored over the list, adding and deleting names, and moving people up and down in his rankings. Finally, worrying to the end, he came up with his lists. He ranked Jack Nicklaus first, followed by Bobby Jones, Ben Hogan, Walter Hagen, Harry Vardon, Gary Player, Sam Snead, Arnold Palmer, Lee Trevino, and, in a tie for tenth, Byron Nelson and Tom Watson.

When it came to the women, Joyce Wethered was first, followed by Glenna Collett Vare, Mickey Wright, Kathy Whitworth, Betsy Rawls, Louise Suggs, Babe Didrikson Zaharias, JoAnne Carner, Donna Caponi, and Patty Berg.

When Anderson studied the lists, he noticed one glaring omission from the men's list—Sarazen himself. Why, he asked, did the first man to win all four of the modern professional major championships—the U.S. and British Opens, the Masters, and the PGA Championship—leave himself out of the rankings? Was it false modesty?

Hardly.

"My wife, Mary, told me I couldn't list myself," Sarazen said.

Later, however, Sarazen told Anderson that if he had ranked himself, he would have been "somewhere around eighth, ninth, or 10th."

Gene Sarazen's game was simple and solid and held up for a remarkably long time.

One day, when he was in his early seventies, he and his longtime friend Ken Venturi agreed to take on two Tour pros who were visiting Marco Island to work on their games under Venturi's watchful eye.

Venturi, then in his mid-forties, was no longer playing much competitive golf, but he and Sarazen proved to be a formidable pair. They won handily, and then retired to the clubhouse for lunch. When it came time for them to leave, Sarazen thanked his opponents for the game and offered them a chance to get their money back.

"Good luck, fellas," Sarazen said. "Come back again when you can play a little better."

Gene Sarazen was all for sportsmanship, but he sometimes wondered whether modern players were taking things a little too far. To Sarazen's way of thinking, sportsmanship was one thing, winning was something else.

"Back when I was playing, if you thought about the other guy at all, you were hoping he'd fall and break both his legs," he said.

It's widely known that Gene Sarazen invented the sand wedge, which revolutionized the game. But another of his innovations was less well publicized.

"One day I was talking with Ty Cobb, who told me he liked to swing a real heavy bat," Sarazen recalled. "I started thinking that if a great hitter like Cobb could groove his swing with a bat like that, maybe I could do the same thing with a heavy club. I called Wilson and had them make up some heavy drivers for me. They worked like a charm, but I could never sell Wilson on the idea."

Sarazen and Cobb became great friends, owing in large part to their competitive natures. Still, even Sarazen paled in comparison to Cobb when it came to the will to win.

"In 1930, I was playing in a tournament down in Florida," Sarazen recalled. "Ty was down for spring training and came by to watch. I was leading by about 15 strokes with nine holes left, so I kind of took it easy. Cobb was furious with me for slacking off. He thought I should have won by 20 strokes."

"I used to take the train from Pelham [in suburban Westchester County] into New York City," Sarazen recalled. "There were some real beautiful showgirls that used to take the same train, and there was one blonde who was just a knockout, but she'd never give me the time of day. Years later, I was out in Palm Springs, and when I finished my round a fellow came down and told me there was a woman who wanted to see me up at the clubhouse. I went up there, and the woman said, 'You don't remember me, but I used to take the Pelham train into New York with you.' She was Bob Hope's wife Dolores—and you can bet I remembered her."

Several years ago a newspaperman, John Steadman, joined Gene Sarazen and two friends for a round of golf on Marco Island, Florida, where Sarazen lived the latter years of his life.

After the round, the foursome retired to the clubhouse. When it came time to order drinks, Sarazen declined to order, explaining that the bar didn't stock his favorite brand of scotch, Old Rarity. In a matter of minutes, the club manager sent an employee to Sarazen's condominium to bring back a bottle.

A few years later, Steadman ran into Sarazen at the Masters and asked if he was still drinking Old Rarity.

"Definitely not," Sarazen said. "I found out they made the stuff in Brooklyn."

When Gene Sarazen made his dramatic double eagle on the 15th hole in the final round of the 1935 Masters, many people believed he all but single handedly put the tournament on the map. Certainly, it gave the Masters an enormous publicity boost, and even today it remains one of the game's most historic shots.

The magnitude of the shot wasn't lost on Sarazen, who went on to win the tournament the following day in a thirty-six-hole playoff with Craig Wood. In fact, he suspected that his friends Bob Jones and Clifford Roberts might be planning to do a little something to commemorate the event. He thought a plaque embedded in the fairway where he played the shot from would be perfect. He asked his caddie, Stovepipe, if he'd heard any rumors.

"Well, Mr. Gene, I sure did see some fellas go down there this morning," he said, pausing for effect. "They filled that divot in just as neat as can be."

Gene Sarazen, then seventy-one, traveled to Troon for the 1973 British Open.

Playing the par-3 8th hole—the "Postage Stamp"—Sarazen made the sixth ace of his career.

"I'm glad they got this one on film," he said. "When I die I'm going to bring it with me and show it to Hagen, Armour, Jones, Ouimet, and the boys."

Gene Sarazen was always a confident, even cocky player. He knew he was good. The other players knew he was good. And he knew the other players knew just how good he really was.

In 1932, Sarazen arrived in England for the British Open at Prince's. The press, knowing that Sarazen was always good for a quote, asked him who he thought would win the championship.

"I have no doubt that the greatest player in the world will win this championship," he said.

And he did. Sarazen beat MacDonald Smith by five strokes.

Gene Sarazen's victory in the 1932 U.S. Open at Fresh Meadow Country Club was highlighted by one of the greatest rallies in golf history—and it was almost marred by an incorrect scorecard.

Sarazen was five strokes off the lead going into the last day, when golfers played thirty-six holes (which they did until the 1965 Open). Sarazen shot an even-par 70 in the morning, then went out and shot a 34 on the front nine in the afternoon. He followed that with a 32 on the back nine for a record-breaking 66 and a three-stroke victory over Bobby Cruickshank and Phil Perkins.

Some thirty minutes after he finished his round, someone noticed that he'd forgotten to sign his scorecard. Sarazen glanced at his card and noticed that his playing partner had marked him for a three instead of a four on the 18th hole.

It might have been the greatest catch in history.

Had he signed for the lower score, he would have been immediately disqualified.

Early in the week of the 1933 PGA Championship at the Blue Mound Country Club in Milwaukee, Tommy Armour told reporters that he thought Gene Sarazen was "all washed up as a championship contender."

One can only imagine the feisty Sarazen's reaction when he picked up the morning paper.

Armour's comment sent Sarazen on a tear through the draw. He beat one Vincent Eldred, 8 & 7, in the first round; clocked Harry "Lighthorse" Cooper, 4 & 3, in the second; pounded Ed Dudley, 6 & 5, in the third; and then met the formidable Willie Goggin in the thirty-six-hole final.

Sarazen came out and shot a 69 in the morning but held just a slim, 1-up lead over Goggin. The afternoon, however, was a different story. Sarazen won three of the first five holes on his way to a 34 and a 4-up lead. He birdied the 32nd hole to clinch the title for the third time, 5 & 4.

"Pretty good for a washed-up golfer," he told the cheering crowd.

Gene Sarazen played on every American Ryder Cup team, from the 1927 inaugural team through the 1937 squad, where he picked up 1½ points as the Yanks breezed to an 8–4 victory over the team from Great Britain/Ireland.

Two years later, when the American captain—Sarazen's old friend and fierce rival Walter Hagen—named the team scheduled to meet the guys from Great Britain/Ireland in November at the Ponte Vedra Club, the thirty-seven-year-old Sarazen's name was among the missing.

Naturally, for someone as competitive as Sarazen, this was too much to bear.

"I can pick ten men right now—myself included—and beat the pants off Hagen's team," he told the press, who gleefully played up the story for all it was worth.

The story had barely made the afternoon papers when Hagen announced that he was taking up the challenge.

As it turned out, Sarazen's challenge proved providential, as England declared war on Germany just a month before the Ryder Cup Matches were to be played.

In the resulting matches, Hagen's Ryder Cuppers edged Sarazen's boys, 7–5, but Sarazen was undeterred.

"The matches were too close to admit defeat," Sarazen said. "We'll play again next year."

And so they did, with Bobby Jones as captain of the Challenge team. He and Sarazen faced two bright young players, Byron Nelson and Jug McSpaden, and lost, but the Challengers won, 8½–6½.

In all, the series of matches raised over $100,000 for war-related charities.

And Sarazen got his measure of revenge.

Back in the 1920s and '30s, when Gene Sarazen and his fellow pros were laying the foundation for the PGA Tour, just because you won a tournament didn't necessarily mean you were going to leave town richer than you arrived. On more than one occasion, tournament sponsors came up empty when it was time to pay off the players. In fact, it happened several times to Sarazen, most memorably one year in Miami.

"I won the old Miami Open, which was a pretty big tournament in those days," Sarazen once recalled. "At the awards ceremony, they gave me a trophy but said they didn't have the $500 first prize. Instead, they offered me an acre of land over on Miami Beach. I told them, no deal. I wanted the cash. We went back and forth, and finally a man in the crowd said he'd give me $500 for the land, and we made the deal."

Sarazen was delighted to get the money, but in the end, the man who bought the property was the real winner. He sold it—at a tidy profit—to the builders of the Fountainbleu Hotel.

Gene Sarazen understood how important it was for a player to have a good relationship with the press, particularly in the days before television began to play such a huge role in covering the game. To that end, Sarazen was always good for a quote or a story that would find its way into the sports section.

"Gene never went to bed at night without two good stories for the writers," remembered the late writer and editor Charlie Price. "He'd have one for the morning papers and one for the afternoon papers. You were never stuck for a story when Gene was around."

Like many players of his era, Gene Sarazen was a master at what are now dismissed as publicity stunts that kept his name—and golf—in the papers.

In 1924, Sarazen was the professional at Briarcliff Lodge in Briarcliff Manor, just north of New York City. One day he found himself involved in what must surely be one of the most bizarre exhibitions of all time.

Sarazen played a nine-hole match against a bait caster. Sarazen would have to hole out on every green, while the bait caster would have to land his lead weight in a thirty-inch target.

As it turned out, the fisherman was amazingly accurate. He beat Sarazen, 4 & 3.

On another occasion, Sarazen became what many people believe to be the first person to play golf under the lights. An association of electrical engineers invited Sarazen to attend their convention and play a par-3 hole they'd illuminated with powerful lamps.

No sooner did the invitation arrive than Sarazen could already envision the headlines. He leapt at the chance and, in true Sarazen fashion, capped the exhibition by making a hole-in-one.

The next day, the story was in all the papers.

Here's a good trivia question: Name the longest-running endorsement deal in the history of sports.

Answer: Gene Sarazen, who signed with Wilson Sporting Goods in 1923 and was with them until his death in 1999.

# SCOTLAND, THE BRAVE

Golf historians can debate the origins of the game, but the Scots insist that it was born on the linksland of St. Andrews, was nurtured by the Scots themselves, and grew to take on the character of these proud people.

That's their story, they're sticking to it, and God help anyone who wants to argue the point. After all, the Dutch can point to a few old prints of guys in black frock coats and funny hats hitting balls along frozen rivers. The Scots can point to a line of British Open champions dating back to the mid-1800s.

When golf began to take hold in America in the late 1800s, it only made sense that the early club professionals would be Scots. One of the most prominent was Willie Campbell, a native of Musselburgh, a town hard by the coast near Edinburgh.

Campbell went to work at The Country Club in Brookline, Massachusetts, in 1894 for the princely sum of $300 a year. Campbell would work at TCC in the spring and fall and would work at the Essex Country Club on Massachusetts' north shore, where many members of The Country Club spent their summers.

One day a Boston writer, anxious to learn the finer points of the game, asked Campbell whether American golfers resorted to Scottish or American profanities on the course.

"Golfers are gentlemen," Campbell said. "They dinna' swear or invoke the name of the Lord in vain."

"Not even when they find themselves in a bunker?" the writer asked.

"Ah, well, in a bunker even a gentleman is human," Campbell said. "And a man wouldn't be human if he didn't swear in a bunker."

One of Willie Campbell's great rivals was another Scottish professional, Willie Dunn, a player of considerable talent and competitiveness. In one match, Campbell's putt came to rest on the edge of the cup. He approached the hole and bent down, staring at the ball and seemingly trying to will it into the cup.

"Willie, are you sure ye na shakin' the ground?" Dunn asked.

"I'm na shakin' the ground," Campbell protested. "I'm just studyin' my putt."

In the 1800s, challenge matches were frequent occurrences between Scottish professionals. One of the most famous was the Great Challenge Match, which took place in 1849 and pitted Allan Robertson and Old Tom Morris against the twins Jamie and Willie Dunn.

The match, with a winners-take-all prize of £400, consisted of three thirty-six-hole matches at three different courses.

The first two matches were split, with the Dunns winning at Musselburgh but losing at St. Andrews.

The third match was played at North Berwick, but the Dunns' luck finally ran out on the 35th hole, when their ball came to rest against a large rock. They lost the 35th hole, then went on to lose the 36th hole, the match, and the £400.

# "SHELL'S WONDERFUL WORLD OF GOLF"

One of the beauties of "Shell's Wonderful World of Golf," particularly the original productions that ran in the 1960s and early '70s, was that the matches were played in exotic locales around the world. One highlight was a match between America's Barbara Romack and the reigning Italian Amateur champion, Isa Goldschmid. It was played in Monaco, where the course's natural beauty was more than complemented by the natural beauty of the wife of the country's ruler, Prince Rainier—Princess Grace.

For those of you who aren't up on their back (sadly, very back) issues of *People* magazine, or who don't have a bazillion cable channels to choose from, Princess Grace was the former Grace Kelly, who was one of the most stunningly beautiful actresses of her time. With precious few exceptions, you could take any of today's glamour-amour-ettes and Princess Grace could give them two a side and close them out early. She was that strong.

Having said all that, you can imagine the reaction when, in the course of filming the Shell match, a Volkswagen Beetle came scooting down the fairway. When it came to a stop, the front doors opened and out stepped the princess and one of her daughters.

"Princess Grace was very, well, gracious," remembers Fred Raphael, the series' producer. "She introduced herself and followed the match for about three holes. When the time came for her to leave, she came over and thanked us.

"'I don't know very much about golf, Mr. Raphael, but I do know a little bit about your business,' she said.

"'I know you do, Your Highness,' I said.

"'I'm afraid you're not going to have a very successful show,' she said.

"'Why is that?' I asked.

"'Because you have six cameras out here and I'm afraid they've all been filming me and not the golf,' she said.

"'That's okay, Your Highness,' I said. 'You're better than the golf.'

"She laughed and then let me in on a little secret," Raphael said.

"'Not as much better as I might be,' she said. 'I'm two months pregnant, but we haven't announced that to the press yet.'"

Her secret was safe with Fred.

When Fred Raphael was starting out with the Shell series, he was the first to admit he didn't know much about golf. But he did have plenty of contacts in New York, and one of them was a director named Lee Goodman, who not only had excellent credentials but also knew a little bit about the game.

One afternoon Raphael and Goodman met Herbert Warren Wind, the celebrated writer who was collaborating on the series, for lunch. In the course of the meeting, Goodman was explaining camera angles and locations to Wind, who listened intently. Goodman was using a shoot he had done with Sam Snead as an example.

After several minutes, Wind asked Goodman where the Snead match had been played.

"Match?" Goodman said. "What match? It was an Alka-Seltzer commercial."

The "Shell's Wonderful World of Golf" series was the brainchild of Monroe Spaght, the president of Shell in the United States. An avid golfer, he was enthralled by the idea of a television show that would highlight golf around the world (and, coincidentally, Shell's worldwide presence).

Since the show was his baby, so to speak, he took a paternal interest in its development—sometimes obsessively so.

"Mr. Spaght was very protective of the show, particularly in our first year," recalls Fred Raphael. "He reviewed every show before it aired. In one case, Herb Wind and I met Mr. Spaght and some executives from [Shell's advertising agency] Kenyon and Eckhart for lunch. Mr. Spaght said he was very pleased with the show we had sent him, but there was just one problem: he said there was a split infinitive in the voice-over and he wanted it removed because he didn't want to 'get letters from eighth-grade teachers across the country.'"

Fine.

Raphael, Wind, and—naturally—the ad guys would have been delighted to remove the offending split infinitive. The problem was, Mr. Spaght didn't tell them just where it was in the show. Finding it proved to be more difficult than anyone could have imagined, and to make matters worse, they were working on a very tight deadline, since the film had to be sent to the network.

Herb Wind screened the film twice, to no avail. It should be noted here that Herb Wind is a Yale graduate who enjoyed many successful years at both *Sports Illustrated* and *The New Yorker*. In other words, Herb Wind would know all about split infinitives.

Desperate, Raphael called in an English professor from Columbia and paid him seventy-five dollars to screen the film. The professor also came up empty, although he did write a note on Columbia letterhead staking his reputation on the fact that there wasn't a split infinitive to be found anywhere.

With time running perilously short, Raphael urged the account executives to call Mr. Spaght with the news that, with all due respect, perhaps he was mistaken.

Now, Mr. Monroe Spaght didn't get to be Mr. Monroe Spaght by listening to account executives tell him he was, well, hearing things.

"They called me back and said, 'If he says it's in there, it's in there, so find it,'" Raphael recalls.

Working on the theory that desperate times call for desperate measures, Raphael called Mr. Spaght's office, only to learn that he was in London for the week.

"I figured that since Mr. Spaght wouldn't see the film and the Kenyon and Eckart guys wouldn't know a split infinitive if it bit them on the nose, I told the production guys to cut the commercials back in and ship the film," Raphael remembers. "While they were editing the commercials into the film, a kid who was cleaning the editing room said, 'There it is.'

"'Where?' I asked.

"'In the commercial,' the kid said."

Life on the road for the Shell series often required more than a little improvisation, as was the case with a match between American pros Carol Mann, Kathy Whitworth, and Sandra Haynie at Thailand's Royal Bangkok Sports Club.

The match would take three days to film, and since the weather was incredibly hot and humid, the women quickly went through their wardrobes. On the eve of the final day, Fred Raphael checked to see what the women were planning to wear the next day. To his horror, he discovered that their outfits would be virtually identical—a disaster for television.

Working quickly, they found alternate outfits for Haynie and Whitworth, but Mann was down to her last change of clothes. Nothing was left to do but take a handful of expense money and head downtown.

"They had tons of beautiful blouses in the stores," Mann remembers. "The problem is, I'm over six feet tall and the blouses were made for Thai women, who are about a foot shorter. I don't think they'd ever seen anyone quite like me. I think we wound up getting a man's shirt at the pro shop. It was a nice shirt, though."

Not surprisingly, some of the courses the Shell series traveled to around the world weren't quite up to the lush standards Americans were used to seeing, and sometimes Mother Nature had to get a bit of a helping hand. That was the case in Greece during a match between Roberto de Vicenzo and Tony Lema.

"The course had just been completed, which was bad enough, but the country was suffering through a brutal drought and the course was absolutely burned out," remembers Fred Raphael. "It was totally brown. You could hardly find a blade of green grass on the fairways. It was going to be a disaster.

"A couple days before we were supposed to begin shooting, I met a colonel in the U.S. Air Force," Raphael went on. "I explained the problem, and he said he had a friend who owned a local crop-dusting company. We quickly made a deal to hire a plane and a pilot, then went out and bought all the green paint we could find. We spent a day spraying the fairways. When we were finished, the place didn't look like Augusta National, but it looked a heck of a lot better than it had before."

And apparently the paint job didn't bother the players. Lema shot a 66 to edge de Vicenzo by a stroke.

The trucks carrying the cameras on the Shell series were heavily camouflaged with leaves and branches so they wouldn't be obvious to the viewers. As a general rule, this worked fine, except for a few memorable occasions.

During the filming of one match in Ireland, a couple of women in the gallery felt the need to answer nature's call and relieve themselves. Since the clubhouse was some ways away, they decided to take advantage of the large, nearby stand of foliage.

This was all well and good until the truck drove off down the fairway, leaving the women exposed to nature and the rest of the gallery.

# SHOW BUSINESS

Frank Sinatra dabbled in golf for a time and even briefly hosted a PGA Tour event in Palm Springs.

Frank Beard won the tournament in 1963. It was his first Tour victory, and the trophy and the check were nice, but there was an added bonus that went with the victory.

"Whenever I'd run into Sinatra, he'd introduce me as his personal pro," Beard remembers. "He loved taking me around and introducing me to all his friends."

Sinatra didn't have either the time or the patience to master the game, but when he did play he was the picture of determination.

One day he was playing in Palm Springs with Gary Morton, who had been married for a time to Lucille Ball. Sinatra hit one poor shot after another and was quickly losing his patience with the ordeal.

"Relax, Frank," Morton said. "The ball doesn't know who you are."

With that, Sinatra picked up the ball, glared at it, and introduced himself.

"I'm Frank Sinatra, the famous singer," he said.

Then he put the ball on the tee and hit it perfectly.

"It was the damndest thing I've ever seen," said Morton.

Even Sinatra's harshest critics are forced to concede that he was unusually generous to his friends. For a time, when he was smitten with golf, he would routinely buy dozens of cashmere sweaters and send them to his friends.

There was one catch: his friends could return them only if they were the wrong size, and if they did return them, they had to exchange them for the same model and color.

As it happens, the color Frank Sinatra was most taken with was a particularly garish shade of orange.

# DENNY SHUTE

Denny Shute is one of those players who never really get the credit they deserve.

Shute came from a family of golf professionals. His uncle Harry was a professional in England, and his father, Herman, was a longtime professional at the Euclid Club in England. Shute held club professional jobs throughout his playing career, which wasn't uncommon during his era. Still, he managed to enjoy considerable success as a player.

Shute won the 1933 British Open at St. Andrews, an accomplishment all the more impressive because it came on his first attempt. After his victory, Gene Sarazen called Shute "the best golfer in the world."

"Denny was a much better player than people give him credit for," remembers Byron Nelson. "He was a quiet, shy man who didn't like to blow his own horn, so to speak. But anyone who won the tournaments he did has got to be good."

Shute was runner-up in the 1939 and 1941 U.S. Opens, but he won the 1936 PGA Championship at Pinehurst, beating long-hitting Jimmy Thomson, 3 & 2. He successfully defended his title the following year at the Pittsburgh Field Club, edging Harold "Jug" McSpaden, 1-up.

As the defending champion, Shute arrived at the 1938 PGA Championship at Shawnee-on-the-Delaware expecting to be

awarded the top spot in the match-play draw. Instead, he was told by officials that since his entry hadn't been received at PGA headquarters, he was ineligible to compete. Shute protested, but the PGA wouldn't budge.

Shute was tremendously popular with his fellow players, and when they learned about his plight, they threatened to boycott the championship. It was an unprecedented stand by the players, but it worked, and Shute was allowed to play.

Despite the controversy, Shute fared pretty well in the championship. He beat Clyde Usina, 3 & 2, in the first round, then dusted Johnny Thoren, 7 & 6, in the second. He wound up losing to Jimmy Hines, 2 & 1, in the quarterfinals.

In the end, the 1938 PGA Championship is remembered for two things: Paul Runyan's 8 & 7 defeat of Sam Snead in the finals and the courageous stand the players took for one of their own.

# DAN SIKES

Dan Sikes was one of the founding forces behind the Senior PGA Tour, which only makes sense, since he had been a successful lawyer from Jacksonville, Florida, before giving up the bar to compete successfully on the Tour.

Prior to a televised match, he was asked what was the biggest difference between playing on the Tour and practicing law.

"About $75,000 more money and a lot less headaches," Sikes said.

# SAM SNEAD

Sam Snead was the leader in the clubhouse in the final round of the 1937 Oakland Open. It was clear that no one was going to catch him, but he wasn't taking any chances. When a photographer from a local paper approached him, he sent the man away.

"It's bad luck to have your picture taken before everyone is off the course and you've got the check in your hand," Sam said.

One of Sam Snead's best friends on the Tour was Johnny Bulla, but it was a friendship that almost proved very costly for Snead.

"Johnny used to promote a ball named the Po-Do, which was sold in Walgreens drugstores," Sam remembers. "They sold millions of 'em, which angered the big equipment makers because it was the first ball sold outside pro shops. It especially angered Mr. Icely, who ran Wilson, because it cut into the sales of their Hol-Hi ball. Mr. Icely did all he could to run John off the Tour, but he wouldn't give in. Finally, one time when I was in Chicago for a tournament, Mr. Icely asked me to come to his office. He told me that Wilson was paying me a lot of money and he didn't want me traveling with John anymore. I looked him square in the eye and said, 'Mr. Icely, I appreciate all you and Wilson have done for me, and you can tell me where to play and what clubs to play, but no one is gonna tell me who my friends are going to be.'"

Sam Snead always insisted that if he was even a halfway decent putter he would have won twice as many tournaments as he did. In truth, he was one of the greatest lag putters in the game's history, in no small part because of his remarkable feel for distance and touch.

One day, when this was brought to his attention, he argued that maybe he was an okay approach putter but "no one ever missed more short putts than I did."

"Maybe that's because no one ever had as many short putts as you did, Sam," countered Doc Middlecoff, Sam's friend and fellow Hall of Famer.

In his defense, Sam did have some memorable problems on the greens—and has the stories to prove it.

"One year this promoter in Charlotte arranged a match between Byron [Nelson] and me," Sam remembered. "We'd play thirty-six holes of stroke play, then thirty-six holes of match play. We came to the last hole of the match play and I three-putted to let Byron into a playoff—then I three-putted the last hole of the playoff to let him win.

"Then there was the 1940 PGA Championship at Hershey Country Club," Sam continued. "I'm playing Byron in the finals, and on the 8th hole I hit my second shot five feet past the hole and six-putted. I wound up losing, 1-down."

Sam Snead came out on tour at a time when there was more than a little gamesmanship being practiced. And no one was better at taking advantage of a rookie than Walter Hagen.

"We were paired one day and we came to a par 3. I wasn't sure what to hit, and while I was trying to decide I noticed Hagen pull a 4-wood from the bag. I had been planning to hit a 3-iron, but when I saw that, I switched to a two. My ball was still rising when it went over the green. Hagen put the wood back in his bag, took out a 4-iron, hit it pin high, and then winked at me and smiled."

Sam Snead was a regular participant on the old "Shell's Wonderful World of Golf" series, in part because having him on a telecast helped ensure solid ratings for that week's show.

In one match, Sam and his opponent met on the first tee, where Jimmy Demaret tossed a silver dollar and asked Sam to call heads or tails. For some reason, Sam forgot to choose.

"I've known Sam for thirty years, and that's the first time I've ever seen him take his eyes off a coin," Demaret quipped.

# LEE TREVINO

Lee Trevino and Hubert Green were paired in the first round of the 1974 British Open at Royal Lytham and St. Annes. In honor of the occasion, Green wore a large, colorful (to say the least) woolen tam-o'-shanter. As they stood on the first tee, waiting to hit their opening tee shots, Trevino couldn't resist commenting on Green's fashion sense.

"That's a nice hat, Hubie," he said. "But if it rains, your head's gonna weigh four hundred pounds."

Lee Trevino grew up in tremendous poverty in Dallas. He lived in a sharecropper's house with his mother and grandfather.

"We had dirt floors, and there was no plumbing or electricity," Trevino recalled. "Hell, I joined the Marines when I was seventeen. The barracks were the first place I ever lived that had running water and lights. I thought I was staying at the Ritz-Carlton."

Another time, Trevino joked about his family's financial straits.

"We were so poor my mother couldn't afford to have me, so the lady next door had me," he said.

Ted Makalena was a close friend of Trevino's, and when he died in a swimming accident, Trevino entered the Hawaiian Open, vowing to donate some of his winnings to Makalena's survivors.

Sure enough, Trevino won the tournament and gave $10,000 of his $25,000 winner's check to Makalena's son, so he could graduate from college and get a start on his adult life.

# THE GREAT TRIUMVIRATE

In the years from 1894 until the outbreak of World War I in 1914, the Great Triumvirate—James Braid, J. H. Taylor, and Harry Vardon—dominated the game. In that period, Vardon won six British Opens, while Taylor and Braid won five times each.

It wasn't surprising, then, that when in 1905 a series of challenge matches featuring the three, along with Scotland's Sandy Herd, was announced it attracted enormous attention in England, Ireland, and Scotland.

The enthusiasm stemmed, in no small part, from the fact that it would pit the Scots, Braid, and the 1902 British Open champion, Herd, against England's Vardon and Taylor. Adding to the excitement was the fact that the matches would be played in both Scotland (at the Old Course at St. Andrews and Troon) and England (at St. Annes and Deal).

The first match, thirty-six holes of running score at St. Andrews, attracted an enormous gallery of more than twelve thousand people. Indeed, the gallery was so large that flags were used to signal which team had won a hole—one color for the English, a second color for the Scots, and a third color in the case of a tie.

To further complicate matters, the fiercely partisan Scots were so vociferous in their support of their fellow countrymen that a shaken Vardon threatened to pull out of the match after the morning round.

At the end of thirty-six holes at St. Andrews, the Scots were 2-up, but the Englishmen more than got their revenge at Troon, where, after thirty-six holes, they were a whopping 12-up.

From there the four headed south to St. Annes, where the Scots rallied and closed the gap to 7-down after thirty-six holes.

Alas for Braid and Herd, their luck ran out when they reached Deal. A huge storm, with heavy, wind-driven rains, swept the course, and by the time the day mercifully ended, Vardon and Taylor had won, 13 & 12.

As they say in the papers, it was closer than the score indicates—but probably not by much.

Harry Vardon, by the way, was an enormous celebrity, both in Great Britain and the United States, where the game of golf was just beginning to catch on.

In 1900, the A. G. Spalding Sporting Goods Company paid him the astonishing sum of £900 to stage a series of exhibitions designed to promote their "Vardon Flyer" golf ball in America.

Vardon and his exhibitions were so popular that when he came to New York City for an afternoon show, the New York Stock Exchange shut down for the day.

# KEN VENTURI

Ken Venturi polished his game under the wise eyes of Byron Nelson and Ben Hogan, which, if you're going to have your game polished, is about as good as it gets.

Early in their friendship, Hogan paid the young Venturi a compliment that gave him a huge boost of confidence.

"In the 1958 Masters, we were all sitting around upstairs in the old locker room having lunch," Venturi recalled. "I was down at one end of the table and Ben was up at the other, near the door. Sam Snead walked in and asked Ben if he had a game for that afternoon. When Ben said he didn't, Sam asked him if he wanted one.

"'Sure, I'll take Venturi and we'll play anyone in the world,' Ben said.

"'I can find an easier game than that,' Sam said."

Ben Hogan died in 1997, just shortly after Ken Venturi's wife, Beau, died from cancer. When Venturi heard that Hogan had died, he called his widow, Valerie, to express his condolences and to tell her he'd be down for the services. Knowing what he was going through with his wife's death, she told him that wasn't necessary. When he insisted, she asked if he'd serve as a pallbearer, and he readily agreed.

"I'm glad, Ken," Valerie Hogan said. "You were Ben's first choice."

Some things never change.

# TOM WEISKOPF

One year at the Masters, tournament officials received a threat on the life of Jack Nicklaus. As is the custom, they informed both Nicklaus and his playing partner, Tom Weiskopf.

When the two players arrived on the first tee, Weiskopf realized that they were wearing similar clothes, so he sent his caddie to the nearby pro shop to buy a different shirt.

"What's up?" Nicklaus asked Weiskopf.

"I'm not taking any chances," Weiskopf said. "I don't want them to get the wrong guy."

# THE WILD KINGDOM

One of the enduring legacies of the British Empire is the popularity of golf around the world. At the height of her power, it was said that "the sun never sits on the British Empire," and that meant there was plenty of time for golf.

Of course, the game was a little more exotic in some of the colonial outposts than it was at, say, St. Andrews or Muirfield. Take, for example, the Delhi Golf Club, in Delhi, India.

The course was carved out of a primordial jungle and is incredibly lush, particularly in the monsoon season. Of course, once a jungle, always a jungle—of sorts. For example, golfers would spot an occasional cobra. But the most enduring problem over the years has been the colonies of rhesus monkeys that populate the course, creating all kinds of havoc.

One of their favorite tricks—although no one could quite fathom why—was racing out to the greens and stealing off with the flagsticks. Naturally, this exasperated the membership to no end. All sorts of solutions were tried, but none worked until they decided on a drastic step: they would cover the lower half of the flagsticks with barbed wire.

Rhesus monkeys are very smart—or at least smart enough to figure out that it was time to move on to an easier game.

Judy Rankin enjoyed a great career on the LPGA Tour, winning twenty-six tournaments before moving on to a successful career as a respected golf analyst for ABC Sports. One reason her career was so remarkable is that for many years she traveled with her young son, Tuey, while her husband, Yippy (probably not the ideal name for the spouse of a professional golfer, come to think of it), tended to business back in Texas. Back in those days, there was no such thing as child care for the players' kids, so finding baby-sitters was very much a catch-as-catch-can proposition.

One year Judy arrived in Portland, Oregon, for a tournament, and when she inquired about child care, she got the name of a person who came with glowing recommendations.

Phew, one less thing to worry about.

Wrong.

When she arrived at the baby-sitter's apartment, everything looked great—until she caught a glimpse of a snake in a terrarium. A very large snake. In fact, a python.

She wisely decided to—as they say—take a drop from this particular hazard, and took Tuey to a place where he'd look more like a kid and less like lunch.

Back in its early days, the Medinah Country Club outside Chicago had an odd feature: it had wild animals about the place. For a time, a camel roamed freely. The club also kept a bear, albeit in a cage.

Eventually, the membership decided the bear and the camel had to go.

The camel because a golf course is no place for a camel.

The bear because it had the bad fortune of biting a kid who reached into the cage to pet it.

Steve Pate can be forgiven if he sometimes wonders if he'll ever get a break—so to speak.

In 1991, Pate was injured in a car accident en route to a dinner for members of the Ryder Cup teams and missed out on the competition.

In 1996, he broke his right hand and wrist in yet another crash and played just three tournaments. Later that year, he chipped a bone in his left wrist when he tripped on a dock.

If all that wasn't enough, insult was added to injury when a deer, being chased by Pate's dog, ran over him, setting back his recovery.

In 1894, The Country Club in Brookline, Massachusetts, hired Scotsman Willie Campbell as its first golf professional. Campbell, a commonsensical sort, took one look at the course and urged the club to purchase a flock of sheep to help keep the grass cut.

Now, at the time there was a sizable chunk of the membership that wasn't thrilled with the notion of golf or of sheep wandering all over the place—or of spending the forty dollars to purchase them.

But the idea carried the day, and for the next nine years the sheep grazed happily, the golfers were delighted with their fairways, the club's horsemen thrilled to the chase—and lamb was a mainstay of the dining room.

Alas, progress arrived in 1903 with the purchase of a steam-powered mower, and the flock was sold.

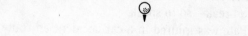

# WIVES, LOVERS, AND OTHER STRANGERS

A sympathetic, understanding, and loving wife is certainly a big plus for a guy trying to make it on tour. But sometimes a wife's love can be—how should we say this?—misplaced. Just ask Rocco Mediate.

Mediate lost in the first round of the inaugural Anderson Consulting World Match Play Championship in 1999, so he did the only logical thing. He called home.

"I'm on my way home," he told his wife, Linda.

"Already?" she asked.

"Yeah, I got killed," he said. "I'm catching a three-fifteen flight."

"That's great. I can't wait to see you," she said.

"Great?" he asked. He didn't think getting blown out in the first round of a tournament with a $1 million first prize was all that wonderful.

"Yeah . . . oh, I mean . . . well, you know what I mean," she said.

While the pressures of tournament competition can easily take their toll on players, in many respects, watching a loved one compete can be every bit as tough—maybe even tougher, since there's not much you can do to help.

In 1966, JoAnne Carner dueled Canada's Marlene Stewart Streit in the finals of the U.S. Women's Amateur Championship. At the end of the regulation thirty-six holes, the match was tied and went into sudden death.

"It was too much for my husband, Don, and Marlene's husband," Carner joked later. "They gave up watching and headed for the clubhouse to drink martinis and wait for the results."

As was so often the case, the result was a victory for Carner—her fourth in this championship.

Winged Foot Golf Club, in the New York City suburb of Mamaroneck, has been a home away from home for its members since it opened in the early 1920s. In fact, for some members, it's more like home than home itself. Take the case of the man who got to the club early, played thirty-six holes, then had dinner and several happy hours relaxing with the guys in the grillroom.

Alas, his reverie was interrupted by a phone call from his wife, who was curious why he was still there and not back home in New York.

"I'm sorry, honey, but the car broke down," he said.

"But you took the train out this morning," she said.

There was a moment of silence.

"Well, that's my story and I'm sticking to it," he said.

Chi Chi Rodriguez was talking with some writers when one of them mentioned the contract Tiger Woods had signed with American Express.

"That doesn't make any sense," Chi Chi said. "He's got so much money, he doesn't need a credit card. They should have asked my wife to endorse their card. She's the world champion of credit cards. Heck, she's the Jack Nicklaus of credit cards."

In 1991, the New York Giants made it into the National Football League playoffs after innumerable mediocre seasons. This, naturally, was a cause for great euphoria among the Giants' long-suffering fans.

One of the playoff games happened to coincide with a January LPGA event being played at Tryall in Jamaica. Two couples from New York happened to be members at Tryall and played in the pro-am. After their round, one of the men told his wife, "The Game's on. We're going up to the clubhouse to watch it. We'll meet you later."

After the men left, one of the wives turned to the other.

"Who does he think he's kidding?" she said. "Harvard and Yale always play in November."

Gene Sarazen was totally devoted to his wife, Mary, although in the early years of their marriage her innocence left him more than a little bemused.

195

"In 1934, I lost the U.S. Open to Olin Dutra by a stroke at Merion," Sarazen remembered. "I was pretty down, but I cheered up when I saw Mary waiting for me at Penn Station.

"'What do you think I did yesterday?' she asked me.

"'I don't know,' I said. 'What did you do yesterday?'

"'I shot an 84,' she said.

"'That's wonderful,' I said. 'What do you think I did yesterday?'

"'I can't wait to hear,' she said.

"'I lost the Open by a stroke,' I said."

Once upon a time, Chi Chi Rodriguez had a girlfriend he thought would make the perfect wife, so he brought her home to meet his father.

The evening went well enough, or so Chi Chi thought until he returned from taking her home.

"What did you think, Dad?" he asked. "Isn't she great?"

"You must never see her again," his father said sternly.

"Why?" Chi Chi asked. "I thought you liked her."

"She's nice, but did you see her fingernails?" his father asked.

"Sure, they're beautiful," Chi Chi replied.

"Of course. That's because they've never washed a dish in her life," said his father. "If she hasn't washed dishes by now, she's not going to start once she gets married. If she won't wash dishes, who knows what else she won't do."

Chi Chi never saw her again.

Arnold Palmer is, to put it mildly, strong-willed. But he met his match when he married Winifred Waltzer.

His early days on tour coincided with the early years of their marriage. He was successful almost from the beginning, but money was tight in those days, and to help make ends meet, they towed a twenty-eight-foot trailer from one tournament to the next.

It should be noted here that Winnie came from a family that, if not rich, was certainly comfortable—not a background that would prepare a young bride for crisscrossing the country in a trailer.

One memorable journey proved to be one memorable journey too many for the young Mrs. Palmer.

The young couple had just finished a tournament in North Carolina and decided to return home to Latrobe, Pennsylvania. Naturally, nothing would do for Arnold but to take a shortcut he knew. Winnie was skeptical, but being young and in love, she said okay.

Along the way, they almost killed a cow in a collision and came close to running off the road twice—on their way up, and then on their way down a mountain. When they reached Latrobe, the young Mrs. Palmer put her foot down.

"That's it!" she said. "I'm never getting back in that trailer again."

"But Winnie . . ." Palmer protested.

"Never," she said.

End of discussion.

# *TIGER WOODS*

If you think Tiger Woods was under a lot of pressure when he won the 1997 Masters, or when he won three U.S Amateurs, or when he outgunned Sergio Garcia to win the 1999 PGA Championship, just consider the pressure he felt at the PGA Tour's 1997 Awards Dinner.

He was awarded the Arnold Palmer Award by the Great Man himself, and as he approached the podium, Palmer stopped Woods in his tracks—and sent a chill through the audience.

"Wait right there," Palmer said, motioning to Woods to pause. "I have something to say. You have an enormous responsibility. When I think of when I started playing this Tour so long ago and how much it's changed, it is amazing. I think we should be thankful, but we should also be careful. Remember how we got here and the guys who helped get us here. You guys are playing for so much money. Always remember that you have an obligation to protect the integrity and traditions of the game. It is important. When I see bad conduct, it truly disturbs me."

Then he signaled for Woods to come stand next to him.

"It's all right here," he said, placing his hands on Woods's shoulders. "The responsibility is all on your shoulders. Protect the game. It's beautiful."

# BABE ZAHARIAS

Babe Zaharias was diagnosed with colon cancer in 1953, and few people expected her to return to championship competition. In the hospital, she prayed for a chance to return to golf, and in 1954, she won an emotional victory in the U.S. Women's Open at Salem Country Club. It was her third Women's Open title.

Sadly, however, her recovery was short-lived. The cancer returned, and she and those around her knew that she had less than a year left to live.

On Christmas Eve, 1955, she was in Fort Worth visiting with friends. As darkness fell, she asked to be driven to Colonial Country Club. When they reached the 2nd green, the Babe, dressed in pajamas and a robe, got out of the car and walked slowly to the green. There, she knelt and slowly ran her hands over the surface, then returned to the car.

"I just wanted to see a golf course one more time," she said.

# INDEX